Walking Shetland

Clan Walk Guides

Walking Shetland

Walking Scotland Series
Volume 7

Mary Welsh
and
Christine Isherwood

First published 1995 by Westmorland Gazette, as
Walks in Shetland
Revised edition *Walking Shetland* published by Clan Books, 2004
This New Edition published by Clan Books 2014

ISBN 978 1 873597 38 5

Text and Illustrations © Mary Welsh and Christine Isherwood 2014

**Clan Books
Clandon House
The Cross, Doune
Perthshire
FK16 6BE**

Printed and bound in Great Britain by
Bell & Bain Ltd., Glasgow

Publisher's Note

Ten years ago, Mary Welsh's original work describing the exciting walking opportunities to be found in the far-flung isles of Shetland was adapted to fit the Walking Scotland series format. Of necessity, this adaptation involved only limited revisions, but recently Mary Welsh re-visited Shetland with her friend and walking companion Christine Isherwood, to re-assess the scene and produce a fully revised text, with all-new maps and illustrations which we offer here as a worthy new recruit for our regularly updated series.

Even with this recent overhaul, the volume may be found to have inaccuracies, caused by changed circumstances or simple error, and readers who spot them are invited to report these to the publishers. Important changes will be posted on the 'updates' page of the Walking Scotland Series website.

The Author's Golden Rules for Good, Safe Walking

- Wear suitable clothes and take adequate waterproofs.
- Walk in strong footwear; walking boots are advisable.
- Carry the relevant map and a compass and know how to use them.
- Carry a whistle; remember six long blasts repeated at one minute intervals is the distress signal.
- Do not walk alone, and tell someone where you are going.
- If mist descends, return.
- Keep all dogs under strict control. Observe all 'No Dogs' notices – they are there for very good reasons.

In all volumes of the WALKING SCOTLAND series, the authors make every effort to ensure accuracy, but changes can occur after publication. Reports of such changes are welcomed by the publisher. Neither the publisher nor the authors can accept responsibility for errors, omissions or any loss or injury.

Contents

Walk Number		Page Number
1	Jarlshof and Sumburgh Head	7
2	Fitful Head	10
3	Loch of Spiggie	13
4	St Ninian's Isle	16
5a	Houss, East Burra	19
5b	Papil, West Burra	21
6	Foula	24
7	Scalloway	28
8	Wester Skeld and Broch of Culswick	31
9	Walls	34
10	Huxter to Sandness Hill	37
11	Papa Stour	40
12	Vementry	44
13	Muckle Roe	47
14	Ness of Hillswick	50
15	Eshaness Lighthouse	53
16	Hamnavoe	56
17	Ronas Hill	59
18	North Roe, North Mainland	62
19	Isbister and Fethaland	66
20	West Sandwick, Yell	69
21a	Gloup, North Yell	72
21b	Breakon, Yell	74
22	Gucher, Yell	77

Walk Number		Page Number
23	Loch of Snarravoe, Unst	79
24	Muckle Flugga, Unst	82
25	Horse Mill of Hagdale and Keen of Hamar, Unst	85
26	Muness Castle, Unst	88
27	Loch of Funzie, Fetlar	91
28	Strandburgh Ness, Fetlar	94
29	Ollaberry	97
30	Lunna	100
31	Out Skerries	103
32	Isbister, Whalsay	106
33	Ward o' Clett, Whalsay	109
34	Setter, Weisdale	112
35	Aith Ness, Bressay	115
36	Kirkabister Lighthouse, Bressay	117
37	Noss	120
38	Mousa Broch	123
39	Six brochs	127
40	Fair Isle	130

Shetland Ponies

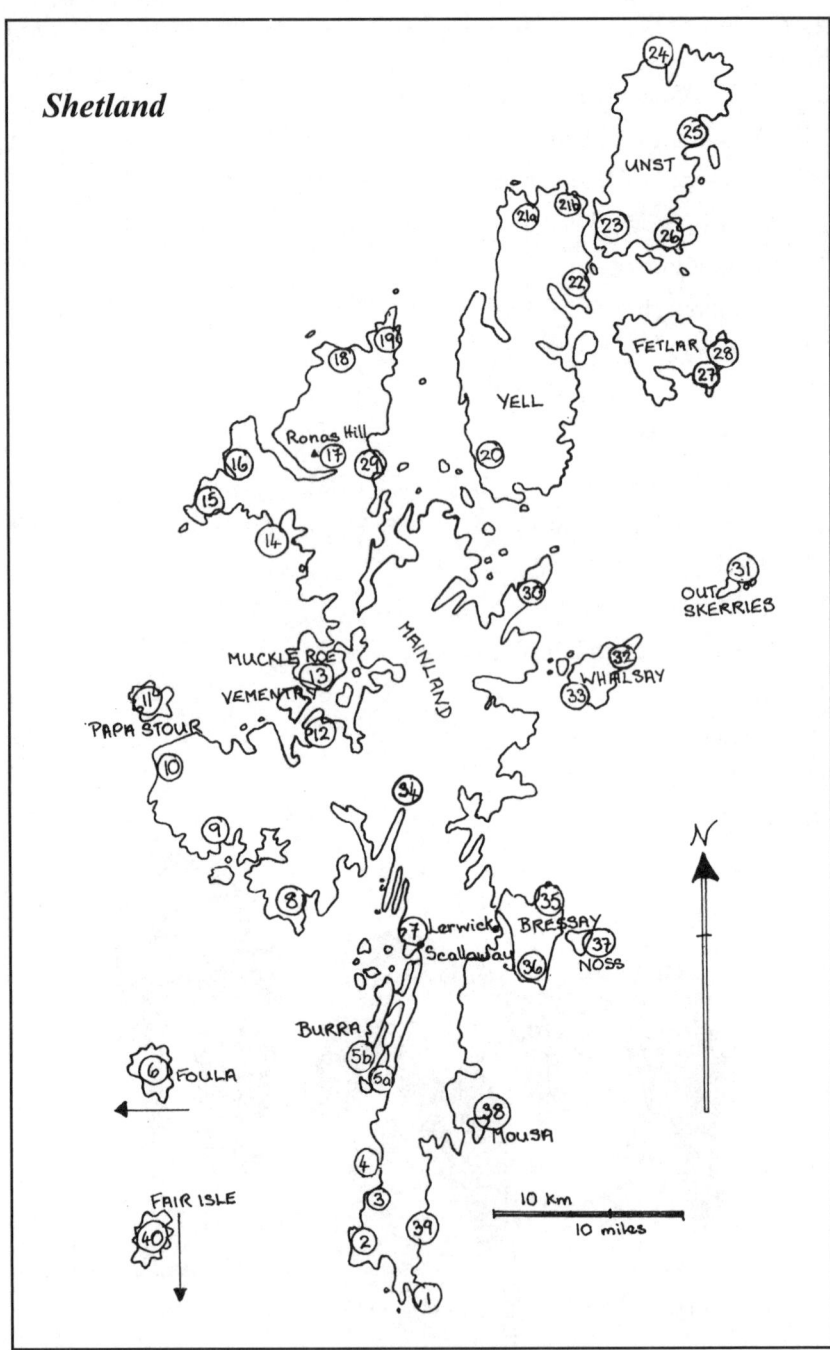

1

Jarlshof and Sumburgh Head

Park in the car park at Jarlshof, grid ref 399097. To access the site use the south-bound A970 from Lerwick and continue through attractive South Mainland in the direction of the airport. Beyond the latter, just after the A-road winds on to Grutness, take the signposted right turn for Jarlshof. Almost immediately turn right into the access track to Sumburgh Hotel. Drive down beside the building, keeping to the right of it and park.

Jarlshof, the unique archaeological site, spanning 3,000 years of settlement, is approached through the car park of the hotel. The site is named after a medieval farmhouse in Sir Walter Scott's novel *The Pirate*. The remains of Jarlshof, which had been buried under sand, emerged after a violent storm in 1905. The site is many-layered, with evidence of occupation from Neolithic times

Jarlshof

through the Bronze and Iron Ages. The Picts and the Vikings were here, and here too a 16th century laird built his mansion.

Shetland's first lighthouse was built by the Stevenson family in 1821. In summer, on either side of the approach lane, the sward is colourful with wild flowers and a nearby pasture is carpeted with pink thrift. To the right are extensive views of West Voe, Scat Ness, over the Bay of Quendale to Garths Ness and, beyond to Fitful Head.

In spring 2014 the **Sumburgh Lighthouse Project** will have fulfilled its aim to conserve the Grade A listed buildings and provide visitor facilities, educational resources and a range of interpretive materials. It aims to tell the story of this fascinating site from Iron-Age Fort to the lighthouse which has protected people and marine life of generations; Sumburgh Head has played an important part in the geological, archaeological and social development of Shetland, and attracts an internationally significant number of breeding seabirds and mammals to the area.

1 From the parking area, take the signed path leading out of the bottom right corner. Walk down beside a pasture and turn right to the Visitor Centre. Spend a wonderful hour or more wandering around the fascinating site. Then return to the entrance. Go ahead, crossing the path from the car park, to stroll the grassy way just above the rocky shore. Carry on through gates, over stiles and ladderstiles, pausing often to enjoy the birds on the shoreline and the several cairns on the green sward. You might spot turnstones running along the tide line, fulmars flying overhead and gannets diving for fish out at sea. At one point the footpath winds round the end of a wall, near to the edge of low cliffs.

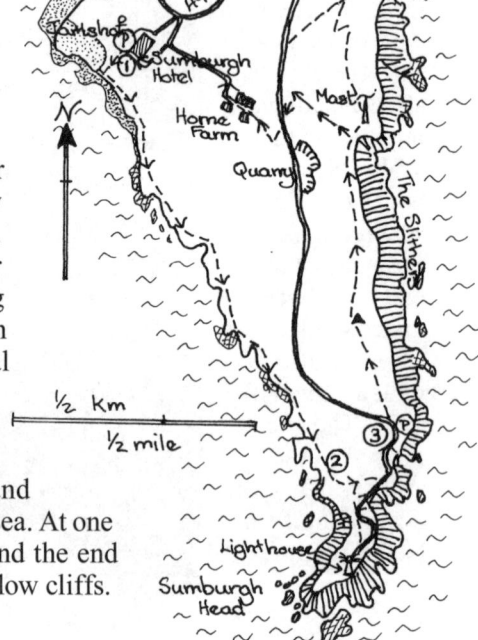

Walk 1

2 With the lighthouse in full view and after the last ladderstile, strike left across the pasture following signs to join the road to the lighthouse. Turn right and as you ascend, peer over the wall on the left, with care. At the right time of the year you might spot puffins standing at the entrance to their thrift covered holes at the top of the near vertical sandstone cliffs. Look for guillemots standing in long lines on white stained rocks, well down the cliffs. Here, too, you might just make out shags sitting on their untidy seaweed nests. Go through the lighthouse gates and wander around the buildings and enjoy the views out to sea from the safe viewing platforms.

Puffins

Thrift

3 Return down the road to reach the small parking area and take the distinct green trod leading out of it. Follow it to the top of Greystane hill, from where there are more superb views. Continue along the delightful high-level path to pass through a broken-down wall. A short way ahead a grassy path descends diagonally to the road below or you may prefer to drop down the easy slope. Turn left along the road for a short way to walk, now on the right, the gated reinforced track leading towards Home Farm. Pass through the farm buildings and carry on to the Hotel.

Practicals

Type of Walk: *Easy exhilarating climb to the lighthouse. Good views. Many puffins at the right time of the year. Just the sort of walk to start you on a great walking holiday.*

Distance:	2½ miles/4km
Time:	2 hours
Maps:	OS Explorer 466/Landranger 4

2

Fitful Head

Park on the wide verge large layby beyond the cattle grid at grid ref 373136 or in the large space on the right nearer to Quendale Mill. Access this by leaving the south branch of the A970 at the sign for Ringasta and Quendale. At Hillwell turn left and continue beyond Gord farm.

Fitful Head, one of Shetland's highest headlands, dominates the very green fertile Quendale Valley. From its summit, 934ft/283m, the views are magnificent.

The **Braer**, the American-owned Liberian-registered oil tanker, foundered on Swart Skerry, below Garths Ness in January 1993, spewing 85,000 tons of crude oil into the sea.

Quendale Mill was built in 1867 by the Grierson family who owned the estate. It began grinding in 1868. In the 16th century the estate was

Quendale Mill

owned by the Sinclair family. The starving Spanish survivors of the Armada's *El Gran Grifon* were brought here from the Fair Isle. It is now open to the public and has a visitor centre and café.

Walk 2

1. From the parking area walk back to the farm just passed. Beyond climb the track on the left. It ascends steadily through sheep pasture and brings you to a large grassy hollow where curlews nest. To your left flows the Burn of Hillwell. Go on ascending through the crowberry and cotton grass of North Gill. At the large bend in the track, take care as you look over the high turf bank to see the ledges of the Nev occupied by fulmars.

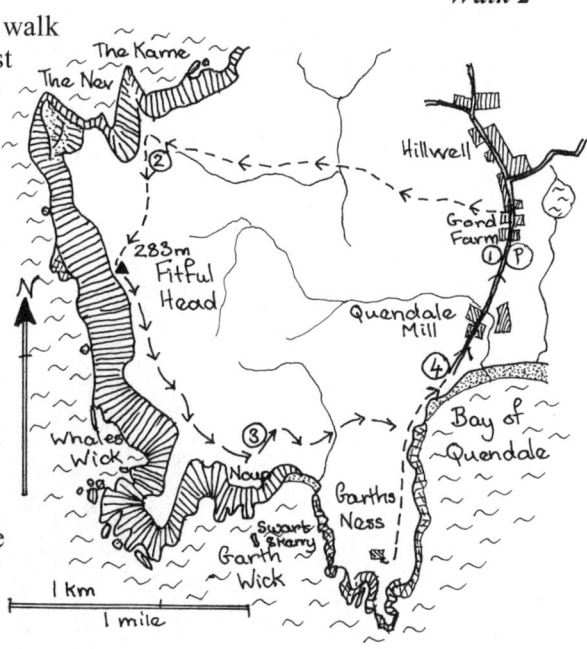

2. Continue steadily, left, uphill, moving into the territory of the great skua. As you go on climbing, pause to look back at the wonderful view of Loch of Spiggie, Colsay, the Bay of Scousburgh, St Ninian's Isle and the receding coastline. Ascend to Fitful Head, and its trig point (920ft/283m). Here you will want to pause and enjoy more magnificent views. Keeping close to the fence, on your right, press on over the crowberry moorland. Ahead you can see Fair Isle and to the west the island of Foula. Carry on down over the crowberry to walk along the fenced cliffs. Look down on the jagged rocks jutting up through the crashing breakers in Whales Wick. The top of Siggar Ness, which overlooks the Wick, is a flat green sward but its sides are almost sheer. Follow the fence as it winds over Noup, covered in blue squill in the summer.

3. Head on down and when it is safe to do so, look down to where The Braer oil tanker foundered on Swart Skerry in 1993. Carry on beside

the fence and wind left with it. Where you reach the junction of two fences above a very steep slope, cross the fence and descend beside the fence on your right. Drop down the next steep slope to a flatter area. Here you pass between the ruins of a large settlement. Cross a small burn and wind on to join a reinforced track. This leads to a narrow road, where you turn left. Dawdle beside the beautiful Bay of Quendale, Shetland's longest beach (nearly a mile) where in 1845 more than 1,500 whales were stranded after swimming ashore.

4 Stroll on along the road to reach Quendale Mill, which you might wish to visit, then carry on to rejoin your car.

Curlew

Practicals

Type of walk: *Stiff climb to the summit. Rough walking by the first fence. An exhilarating, demanding walk with tremendous views throughout.*

Distance: 5½ miles/9km
Time: 5 hours
Maps: OS Explorer 466/OS Landranger 4

3

Loch of Spiggie

Park in the car park overlooking the Bay of Scousburgh, grid ref 372179. To access this, leave Lerwick heading south on the A970 and then take the B9122, a narrow road with passing places, on the right, at grid ref 399224. Just beyond Scousburgh, at South Scousburgh, take the first right turn towards the loch to turn right into the signposted car park.

The **large shallow loch** was once a sea inlet, the Voe of Lunabister, however it has been isolated by the natural formation of sand dunes. The lochs of Spiggie and Brow, together with the adjacent marshes, have been designated a SSSI by Scottish Natural Heritage. The RSPB owns 205 acres of this delightful area. The loch is famous for trout fishing and is also one of the most important in Shetland for its wildfowl. Of special interest are the whooper swans, considerable numbers of which pass through during their migration south in late autumn. In spring many long–tailed ducks gather to roost and can often be seen displaying.

Boats in nousts, Bay of Spiggie

Whooper Swans

Walk 3

1. Start your walk around the loch in an anti-clockwise direction. As the road curves, pass through a gate on the right to visit Spiggie beach with its lovely red sandstone cliffs and stacks, where in summer thrift and sea campion thrive on the steep faces. Look for ancient nousts cut into the grassy hinterland of the sandy beach, some occupied by modern day boats. Return to the road to walk right past Spiggie House. Continue on. Ignore the way to the settlement of Noss on the right. Head on past Symblisetter and then below the slopes of Noss Hill. Pause here to look back at the island of Colsay beyond the dunes.

2. At Bakkasetter look right for three turf-roofed buildings, dating from the 19th century, close by the modern farmhouse. Just beyond, look left to see a burnt mound. Where the road swings right, pass through a gate on the left to walk ahead over a pasture, to the next one. Cross over more pastures with Loch of Brow below to the left. Look for an island connected to the

Sea Campion

land by a causeway of stones, which are slightly submerged – this was once a broch. Continue to the right of a picturesque ruined crofthouse and some old outbuildings and on to pass through a gate in the wall. To the right stands a striking white church with a castellated tower and red roof, Dunrossness Baptist Church, built in 1816.

3 From the gate in the wall stroll ahead to a gate in the wall of the farmhouse, where you turn left to head on over pasture, with Loch of Brow still to your left. Go through the gate in the next wall and follow the footpath to cross clapper bridges over two small burns. Press on diagonally left to go through the next wall by another gate and on along the grassy pasture below heather. Keep to the right of a small house and beyond the gate join a road and go ahead, ignoring the right turn. At the end of the road pass a low white house. Go through two gates and then walk diagonally right. Pass to the right of a farm to join a metalled road.

4 Bear left and at the T-junction left again. Carry on along this quiet way to the end of the road. Climb a stile to the left of a house to see the remains of a broch. Look for the grassy ramparts, part of which have been cut away to build a modern-day house. In the centre is a hollow in which would have stood a double-walled tower. Return to walk right of the house, passing through two gates. Turn right and drop down the slope, with a fence to the right, to another gate. Beyond walk on to cross a narrow burn then strike diagonally, uphill, and pass to the right of a short stone wall that projects into the pasture. Go through the gate at the end of the wall and ahead are pleasing views of Loch Spiggie, Spiggie Bay and Scousburgh Bay.

5 Keep left of a house to join a narrow road and walk on. Pass through the small community of Souther House and at the T-junction turn left beside the loch. Away to the right are the magnificent dunes that have built up to form the wide ayre. Stroll on to rejoin your car.

Practicals

Type of walk: *Easy walking all the way. Some pastures may be wet. An enjoyable inland walk, with a glimpse of the sea from a lovely beach. Some walking on narrow almost traffic-free roads.*

Distance: 5 miles/8km
Time: 2–3 hours
Maps: OS Explorer 466/Landranger 4

4

St Ninian's Isle

Park at Bigton, next to the tombolo, grid ref 374208. To access this follow the A970 from Lerwick and turn right onto the B9122 for Bigton. Take the second right turn for the township, then where the road turns right look for the sign directing you left, then immediately right, for the car park.

St Ninian's Isle, once tidal, is now linked to the mainland by a magnificent shell-sand tombolo (isthmus). It is unique, not only in Shetland but also in Great Britain, because it is composed of about 4 feet of sand lying on top of shingle; other tombolos consist of only gravel or shingle and are generally called ayres. It is a ¼ mile long and has been built up by wave action from opposing directions – Bigton Wick to the north and St Ninian's Bay to the south.

It is believed the site of the **ruined church** was used for domestic occupation from the first century BC to the third century AD and then it became a burial ground where people were interred in a crouching position – short cist inhumation. After that it was used as a Christian burial ground where bodies were placed in long cist and aligned

Tombolo, St. Ninian's Isle

approximately east-west. It is thought that in AD 800 Norse raids might have interrupted the use of the site and that a family hoard of Pictish silver was buried in the church for safety during such dangerous times.

All above was followed by **Norse Christianity** and a larger chapel was built above the first. This was enlarged in about the 12th century. The decay of the church probably came with the Reformation. The island was still populated until the 1700s.

In July 1958, a **Shetland schoolboy** was working on the excavation of the site and he found the box of Pictish silver objects. The treasure is now held in the Royal Museum, Edinburgh. Fine replicas can be seen in the Shetland Museum in Lerwick.

As you walk with great care along the cliffs and look onto sheer faces of other cliffs watch out for **rabbits climbing** almost vertically from the shore upwards.

1 Descend the track to the shore to dawdle across the glorious tombolo. Here, in the right weather conditions, the turquoise water laps gently on both sides. Once across climb the sandy slope where you can see the roots of marram grass binding the sands. Keep left around the

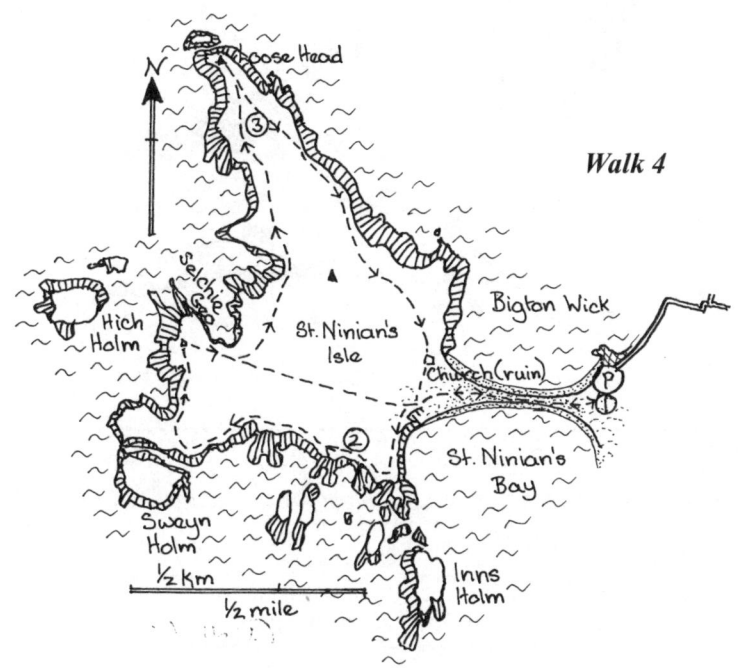

Walk 4

17

lovely cliffs where in spring long stemmed squill grows in profusion. From the most southerly promontory on the island, you can look across to Inns Holm and Coar Holm, surrounded by spectacular reefs and stacks.

2. Wind on round close to the cliff edge and at the wall, climb the ladderstile to continue on the lovely trek. Cross the fence by a step stile. Continue past Sweyn Holm where you might spot grey seals. Take care at Longa Berg, noticing the hidden edge. Climb up to a small stone building, then follow the distinct path inland, then left. Dawdle round Selchie Geo, where you might, at the right time of the year, see puffins preening on ledges, among the fulmars, then disappearing into the dark crevices of the layered sandstone. Walk on towards Loose Head and pause to enjoy the marvellous view.

3. Begin your return southwards by descending towards the cliffs to walk above them to a step stile over the fence. Walk uphill to a ladder stile over the wall. Beyond stroll down over the sward to the ruins of the 12th century church. After your visit, walk right from the site to descend to the tombolo.

Fulmars

Practicals

Type of walk: *Easy walking. A must for all visitors to Shetland.*

Distance: 3 miles/5km
Time: 2 hours
Maps: OS Explorer 466/Landranger 4

5a

Houss, East Burra

Park well up on the grass at the end of the road at Houss, grid ref 377311. Do not obstruct the turning space. Access this by the B9074, south from Scalloway. Turn left at Hamnavoe and continue to Bridge End. Bear left through East Burra to reach Houss.

Look for **turnstones** on the Ayre where you might spot several birds using their pick-axe beaks to turn over stones before pouncing on sand-hoppers, small crabs or molluscs. Their variegated plumage makes them almost invisible, providing useful protection.

Turnstones

Fitful Head from Ward of Symbister, Houss

1 Pass through the gate at the east side of the turning space and walk down a wide grassy track to a gate onto Ayre Dyke, generally covered

19

with a mass of flotsam thrown up by the tide. At the end of the Ayre ascend the grassy track with pastures sloping upwards on either side. At the top you can see Houss Ness stretching ahead. Continue past a ruined crofthouse and go on to a gate in the fence on the right where the track ends. Go diagonally up the pasture, through another gate, and follow the fence towards the shore strolling along sheep trods to reach the west side of this delightful grassy finger of land. Towards the headland the cliffs become sheer and here many birds nest. Look for a splendid natural arch and then over the sea to the island of Havra.

2 Follow the craggy, indented coast round to begin your return along the east side of this narrow strip of land. Across Clift Sound rear the steep grassy Hills of Clift. Climb the slope to the high point of the peninsula, marked by a large boulder. Enjoy the fine view, then cross a fence and continue along the delightful ridge over short heather. Go over another fence to a signpost. Follow the waymark posts downhill over two stiles.

After the last post turn sharply left to a gate, which leads onto the track taken earlier. Carry on across the Ayre and climb the slope to the parking place.

Walk 5a

Practicals

Type of walk: *Easy and charming.*

Distance: 2½ miles/4km
Time: 2 hours
Maps: OS Explorer 466/Landranger 4

Papil, West Burra

Park in the good car park at the road end beyond Papil, grid ref 368310. Access this from Scalloway using the same route as Walk 5a. At Bridge End follow the road as it swings right and then left to where the metalling ends beyond Papil.

The name **Papil** means priests and this was believed to be an early Christian site. The 'Monk's Stone' dug up in Papil added to this belief. The stone is now found in the Shetland Museum. It was replaced by a replica in 2000.

Stacks are vertical columns of rock in the sea, near to a coast. They are formed when a headland is eroded by a crashing sea, the force of the water weakening cracks, eventually causing the cliffs to collapse forming free-standing stacks or small islands.

Crofthouse Museum, Papil

Walk 5b

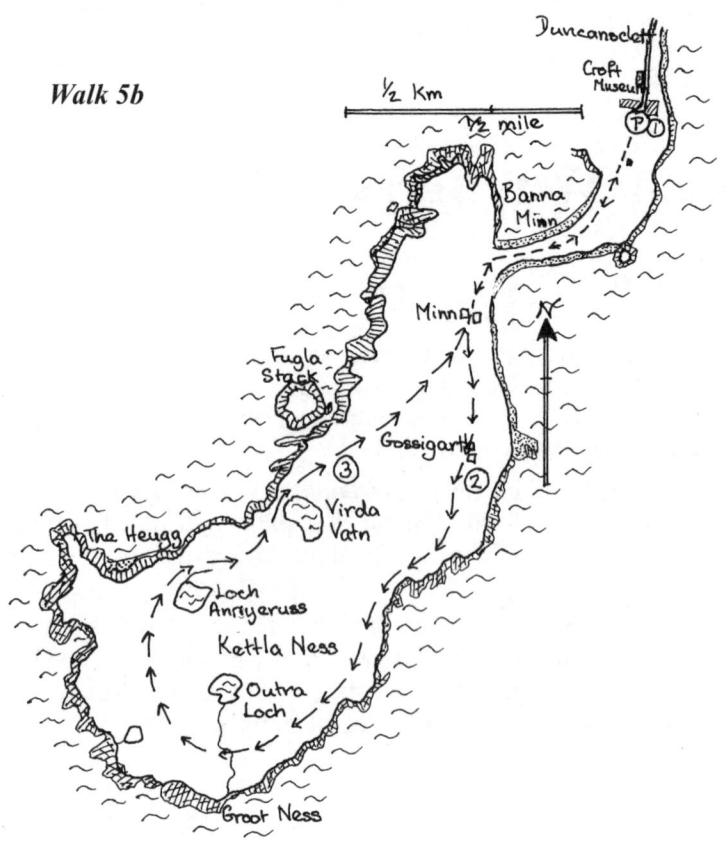

1. From the parking area walk back 55yds/50m to look at the restored croft house and outbuildings, now a museum. Then return to the car park and go through the gate signed 'Access track and Path to Beach'. Descend the hill to go on along the reinforced track over the Ayre. From here you might see seals basking on the rocks in West Voe. Beyond the causeway, continue ahead to pass behind a cottage at Minn. Go through the next three gates to come beside another crofthouse. Carry on to a gap in the wall and then a gate in a fence onto the heather moorland of Kettla Ness.

2. Bear left towards the low cliffs, and stroll on the lovely coastline in a clockwise direction. Look for natural arches and huge sea stacks some of which are covered with grass and others, in summer, with white sea campion stretching down to sea level, where pairs of black guillemots

22

bob about on the water. As you walk round the headland, there is a spectacular view to the north along the west coast of West Burra. Press on past Outra Loch and then Loch Annyeruss, keeping both to your left. Stride on to pass Virda Vatn, a larger loch.

3 Keep on along the pleasing way to climb a stile over a fence from where you can spot the Ayre. Head across a wettish area and pass through two gates to reach the causeway. Cross and climb the track to return to the parking area.

Black Guillemot (Tystie)

Practicals

Type of walk: *Easy walking. A delightful cliff walk with much to see.*

Distance:	4 miles/6.5km
Time:	2–3 hours
Maps:	OS Explorer 466/Landranger 4

6

Foula

Inter-island ferries from Walls Pier on the West Mainland serve Foula three times a week. This is not a day service or a car ferry and journey time is 120 minutes. Booking essential. Contact 07881 823732.

Chartered air service, Direct Flight, operates several times a week from Tingwall Airport, just outside Lerwick. This service provides for a day trip with a few hours to explore. Contact www.directflight.co.uk/shetland.html

Foula is the most westerly island in the Shetland group. It is dominated by high hills and precipitous cliffs. The Sneug, 1,373ft/418m high, provides a wonderful viewpoint. The Kame, 1220ft/372m is awe-inspiring and is the second highest cliff in Britain. If the weather is kind you may be able to tackle a walk over these high precipitous cliffs. If not and it is misty or raining, enjoy this excellent dramatic coastal ramble. Walks on Foula cannot fail to remind you of the derivation of the name from the Norse, Fugl ey, meaning bird island.

Gaada Stack, Foula

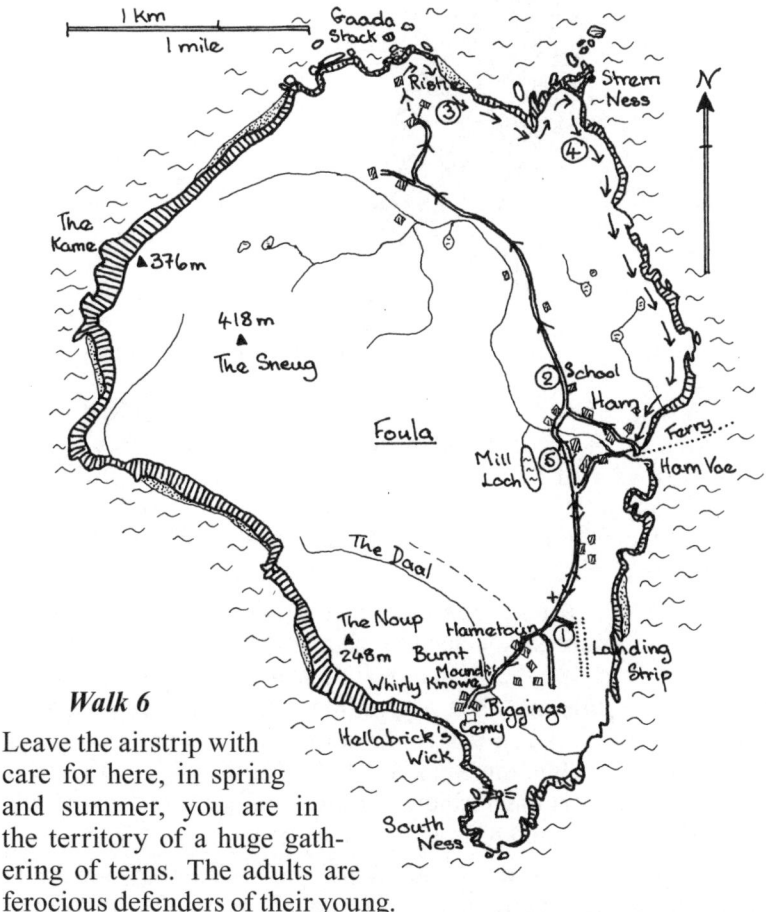

Walk 6

1. Leave the airstrip with care for here, in spring and summer, you are in the territory of a huge gathering of terns. The adults are ferocious defenders of their young.
At the T-junction, turn right, north, along a narrow road past Baxter Chapel, which you might like to visit. Stroll on to pass Mill Loch from which, in late spring, a tiny stream emerges, its banks lined with marsh marigolds and milkmaids. Continue through the tiny settlement of Ham, (Da Toon o Ham), where you will find the post office along a short track on the right. Descend the steepish hill and climb towards the school. Here a narrow road comes up from the harbour, and this is the road you will walk if you travel to the island by boat.

2. Continue on the 'main road' until it veers a little left and then at Da Height, swing right. As you breast the brow ahead enjoy a dramatic view of Gaada Stack, with its impressive natural arch. Carry on

Twite

downhill and then strike across the pasture to pass Da Ristie, which provides simple accommodation for young people. Beyond, walk with care as you approach the immense limestone cliffs. Stand still as you watch the many puffins returning to their burrows with food for their young and the kittiwakes streaming through another magnificent arch.

3 Return right and then continue east along the cliffs for a closer view of the impressive Gaada Stack and then stroll on. Keep above the pebble beach, where great rollers can come crashing in. Cross a fence by a stile and then begin the walk round Stremness. Look back into the first geo to see the fantastic diagonal patterning of sandstone and schist inter-banded with granite. Notice the intensely weathered cliffs at the northern extremity of this promontory, where a multitude of jagged granite 'teeth' project.

4 Continue round the dramatic stiled coast, watching out for grey seals. Inland grows crowberry and heather, spangled with tormentil. This is the territory of the great skua, possibly the largest colony of this species in the world. Pass several ruined crofthouses where the ubiquitous fulmar nests. As you near Ham Voe keep outside the fence until you reach the harbour, where you might spot the ferryboat lifting off supplies by crane. Walk up the harbour road and turn left.

5 Press on the quiet narrow road to pass the airstrip. Head on to the tiny hamlet of Hametoon. Just before you cross the burn look right for the large burnt mound, Whirly Knowe, a reminder of much earlier settlement of the island. Look upstream of the burn to see the ruins of a watermill and above, on the slope, many ruined crofts.

Carry on to the last house, Biggings, and turn left, just before it, to visit the cemetery with its ruined church and many old gravestones. Continue to the edge of the cliffs to look over Hellabrick's Wick and right to see the sheer cliff face of The Noup. Then return towards the airstrip, or the harbour.

Great Skuas (Bonxies)

Practicals

Type of walk: *An interesting island for walking though sad to see so many ruins.*

Distance:	8 miles/3km
Time:	4–5 hours
Maps:	OS Explorer 467/Landranger 4

7

Scalloway

Park in Burn Beach car park, Scalloway, grid ref 403394.

Scalloway was once the capital of Shetland. It is the second largest settlement and the largest port on Shetland's Atlantic coast. Its harbour, full of fishing and oil rig servicing vessels, is dominated by the ruined castle, which was built in 1600 by forced labour for Patrick Stewart as his principal residence in Shetland. He was Earl of Orkney and Lord of Shetland, a half-brother to Mary Queen of Scots.

Patrick Stewart's alleged oppressions have become part of the local folklore. It was said that the mortar of the castle was **mixed with human blood and eggs**. He was executed in 1615 and his castle quickly became ruinous. In 1653 it served temporarily as a garrison for Cromwell's troops.

Scalloway Castle

Walk 7

1 Walk along New Street, with the harbour to your right, to visit the castle (key from Scalloway Hotel, or from the museum during opening hours, April – September). You might also have time to visit the museum just uphill from the castle. Return along New Street, harbour to your left, to pass the splendid Old Haa, once the laird's house. Go straight ahead past a garden of trees

planted in the last century by landowners and prosperous fish merchants. Turn left again to walk beside the wooded area, then go right along Berry Road to where it becomes a narrow metalled way.

2 At Berry farm, pass through a gate onto a reinforced track. Follow it as it swings left and then right round some outbuildings. Go through another gate and continue to the next. Beyond, walk on ignoring the track on the left. Ascend the steadily climbing way and pass through the next gate. Once over the brow enjoy the splendid view of the island of Hildasay and many smaller islands.

3 As you descend look right across to the pretty Loch of Burwick where bogbean flourishes and redshanks nest. Beyond is the site of an ancient homestead. Closer to the loch, lie two burnt mounds. To visit them, cross the moorland to your right and pass through a small gate in the wall. Cross the outflow stream and go on beside a small feeder stream of the loch until you reach the two sites. Here, the stream would have provided the water needed to cook the ancient people's meat and fish. Go back to follow the outflow stream as it heads for the sea and look for the remains of two watermills.

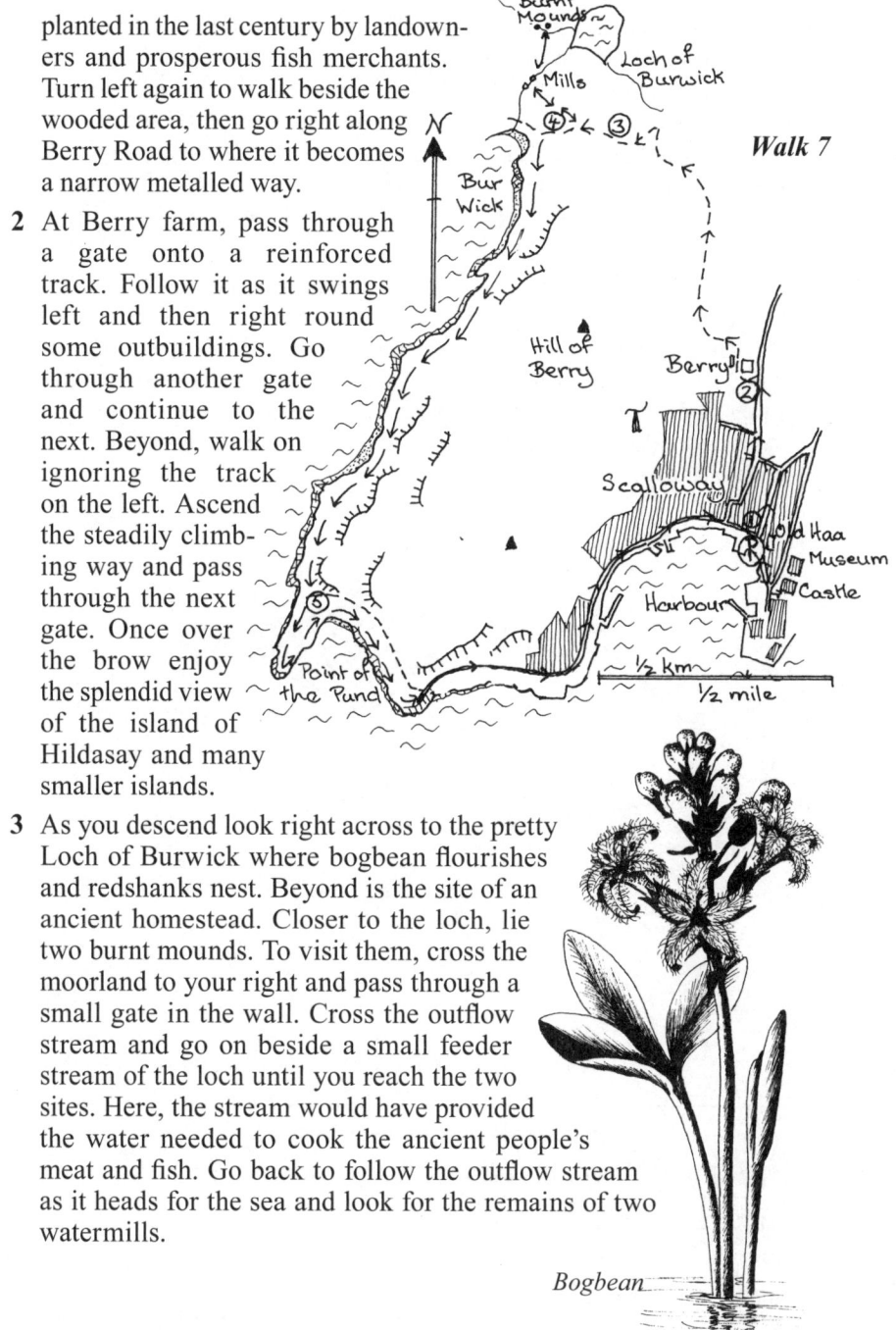

Walk 7

Bogbean

4 Return across the heather to the gate onto the track and walk downhill to the Bay of Bur Wick. Turn left to cross the wall and begin your walk along the pleasing shallow cliffs, the turf in summer sprinkled with numerous wild flowers. Out to sea you can see Hildasay where granite was quarried. Take care as you continue on the generally easy way. Ahead across the waters of the voe you can see the houses of Hamnavoe, the lighthouse on Fugla Ness and the bridge from Trondra to Burra.

5 Cross a track and carry on round the small promontory, Point of Pund. Stand by the light at the entrance to East Voe of Scalloway to see the startlingly green island, Green Holm, an island of limestone, hence the greeness. Scalloway is built on parallel bands of gneiss, schist and limestone. Walk on round the point and across the beach of Pund Voe to head on along the shallow cliffs. Eventually leave the shore and join the road leading into Scalloway.

Redshank

Practicals

Type of walk: *An easy walk with lots of contrast.*

Distance: 4 miles/6.5km
Time: 2–3 hours
Maps: OS Explorer 466/Landranger 4

8

Wester Skeld and Broch of Culswick

Park near to the Wesleyan Church at Wester Skeld, grid ref 296439. Access this from the A971 by the B9071 at Park Hall, a mile west of Bixter. Follow the B-road through the attractive settlement of Easter Skeld and after one-mile take a left turn, signed for Wester Skeld.

The striking red sandstone **Broch of Culswick**, about 10ft high at its tallest point, stands on top of a massive platform of rock. Much rubble has fallen into its centre, however a solid lintel stone still stands over the entrance; this too is partly filled with rubble. Enjoy the superb views all around, including Fair Isle, Foula, and Fitful Head.

Brock of Culswick

Walk 8

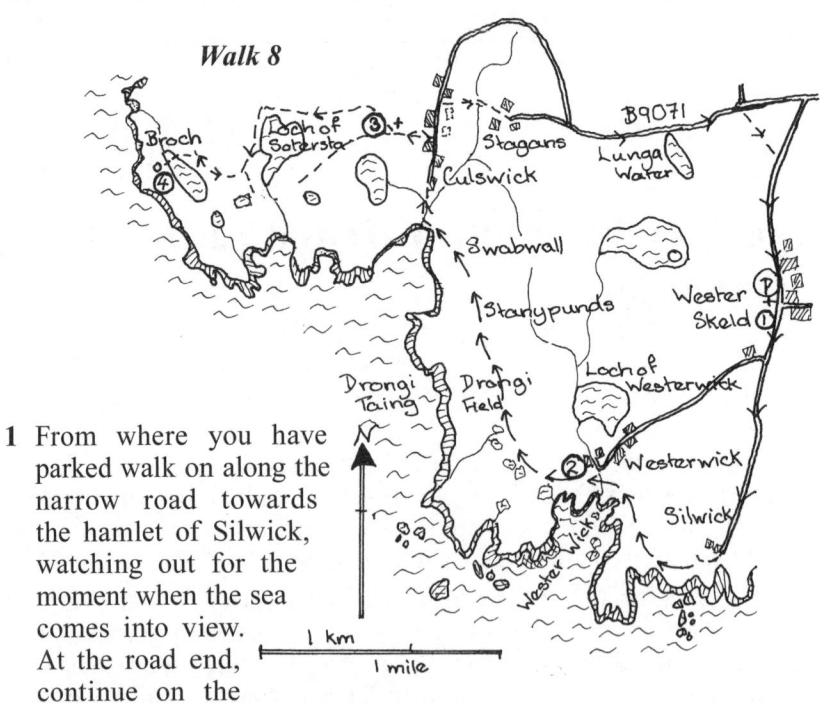

1. From where you have parked walk on along the narrow road towards the hamlet of Silwick, watching out for the moment when the sea comes into view. At the road end, continue on the reinforced track to leave it, left, through a gate. This gives access onto the headland where the turf, in summer, is dotted with wild flowers. Take care at the edge of the cliffs as you look along the jagged coastline where fulmars continually leave and return to their nesting ledges on the stacks. Below shags hang out their wings – to dry or to help them digest their food. Turn right and climb the slope, now with majestic stacks below to your left. Stride on the glorious way leading to the spectacular bay of Wester Wick and descend to a tiny valley.

2. Climb the steepish slope ahead and go on over fences as you come to them. At a wetter area, choose the driest way between peaty pools. Pause to enjoy a fine view of Foula. Press on, slightly away from the cliffs, over the rolling pastures of Drongi Field, Stanypunds and Swabwall. Then descend the steep slope to cross the boulder-strewn narrow beach at Culswick to a gate at the far side. Turn right to walk a narrow road. At Stagans (see map) turn left along a track signed to Culswick Broch. Where it divides by the tiny

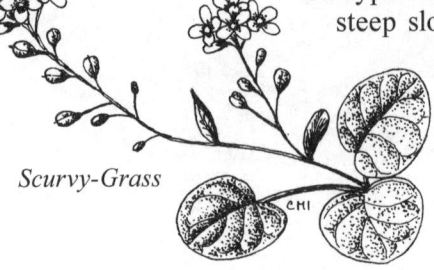

Scurvy-Grass

Methodist Chapel take the signed right branch and follow it over the moorland.

3   Keep north of the Loch of Sotersta in the valley below and carry on to come towards the Loch of the Brough with the broch and its ramparts beyond. At the end of the track, go downhill to cross the causeway and through the gate in the fence beyond it to begin your ascent to the broch, where you will want pause.

4   Return to the foot of the ramparts and rejoin the track. Stride right for nearly a mile to pass the tiny Culswick Methodist Chapel, just before a gate. Dawdle on the track to reach the narrow road once more and turn left. Before the next inhabited house, on your right, pass through a gate on your right. Follow the fence, on your right, down the hillside to another gate. Beyond bear left to cross a tractor bridge and climb the slope to walk left of a wall. Continue along a farm track and then the on-going metalled road (B9071). Walk on uphill. Ignore the left turn and head on the narrow road over the heather moorland. Pass Lunga Water on your right. At the next left turn, walk right, keeping to the left of a fence to join a peat track that cuts off the corner to Wester Skeld. Turn right and walk on to where you have parked. If the short cut is too muddy then continue on the B-road and take the next right turn to Wester Skeld.

Ringed Plover

Practicals

Type of walk: *Good walking, particularly over the close-cropped turf of the cliffs. This is a lovely quiet walk but you will need to use your map regularly. Do not attempt in mist. Pick your way round any peaty pools.*

Distance: 8½ miles/13.5km
Time: 4–5 hours
Maps: OS Explorer 467/Landranger 4

9

Walls

Park close to Walls garage and the public hall, in the middle of the village, grid ref 243495. Access this by a branch of the A971 from Lerwick, which heads south at grid ref 260512.

The name **Walls** is a corruption of the Norse word 'vass'. It means the 'place of the voes'. It is a small village, its sturdy houses spread spaciously around a glorious natural harbour.

When walking close to Burrastow Hall look for the baronial hall built by Herbert Anderson, a Yorkshire millowner. Up above the hall, on the cliffs, stands a **look-out tower**. Legend has it that it was used by the millowner to watch his fishing boats come into the harbour, checking that none of his employees dropped off some of their catch along the coast. He wanted all his fish.

Cairn, near Burrastow

1. Walk south-west to pass the memorial cross on your right. Go over a small stream, which leaves the Loch of Kirkigarth and flows into the harbour. Turn left into Pier Road and continue past the church, a small jetty and a pier. Go on to cross two cattle grids and bear left along the shore to pass below a bungalow. Beyond the next gate, look for a concrete slab on the right, all that remains of a herring station. Beyond the next gate, stroll on with a good view to your left of the small island of Linga. Continue on to join a reinforced track, which leads to a white house at the point, and bear right before it. Carry on over intervening fences and then curve right along the shore below a cottage at Stapness, where you might spot wheatears flitting about the rocky outcrops.

2. Stroll on and then wind inland, along the edge of Loch of Vadill, to join a narrow road and turn left to walk on, ignoring the next left turn. Look, as you go, for circular stone structures, known as plantiecrubs, where crofters raised their cabbages from seed safe from hungry sheep and the destructive wind. On the right, on a green slope stand the remains of a fine crofthouse, the fresh green grass contrasting sharply with heather, evidence that the land was under cultivation for a long time. Ignore the right turn to Dale and stride on, winding on round left, along the west side of Lera Voe. As you walk you have a good view of Vaila Sound and maybe the Foula ferry plying towards Walls. There is a tower above the cliffs at the end of Vaila.

Common Seal

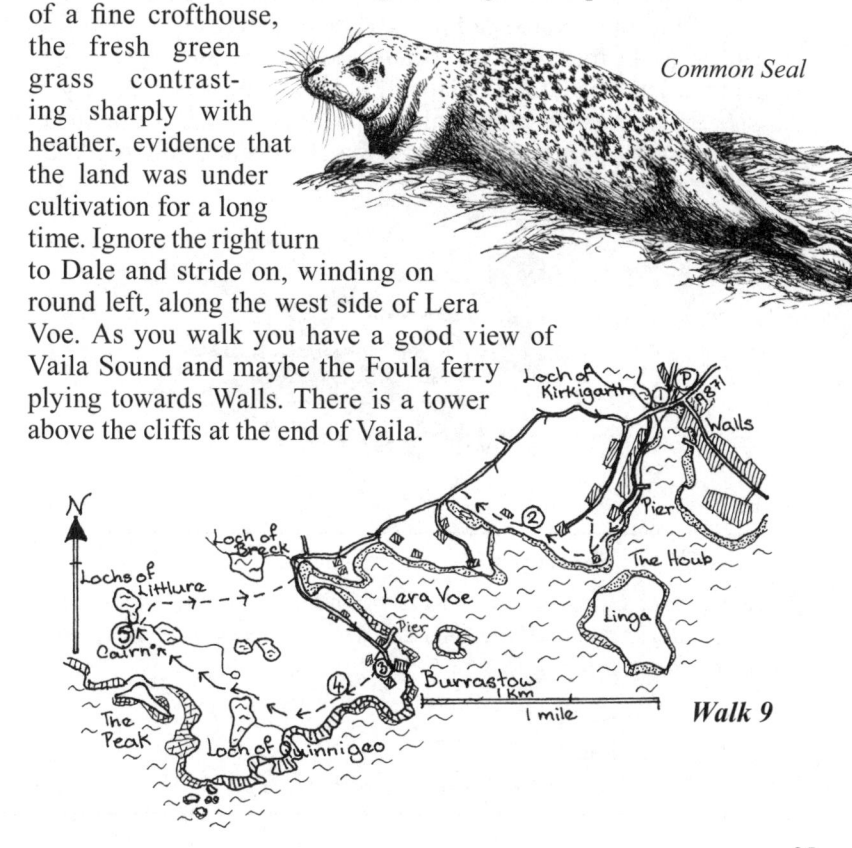

Walk 9

3   The road ends at Burrastow Hotel, a fine 19th century house. Bear right just before the entrance gate, keeping to the right of the wall. Continue past the access track to Burrastow Lodge, then pass through the signed gate ahead and swing left. Ignore the next gate and walk to the right of the wall. From here you have a dramatic view of the baronial hall built by Herbert Anderson, a Yorkshire millowner.

4   Carry on along the cliffs, with care, to a wall and follow it right until you reach a gap. Beyond continue with a fence to your right to pass through a gate in the right corner. Pause here to look down on a secluded pebble beach and ahead for a glimpse of the Loch of Quinnigeo. Bear right to walk round the top, north, of the loch. Climb the next two fences beyond, walking ahead through heather. Then climb steadily to a cairn on the hill ahead, from where there is a spectacular view of great white breakers crashing on the jagged rocks of The Peak.

5   Drop down from the hill to the track you can see below and turn left. Walk on and follow the track as it winds right, passing between the Lochs of Littlure before heading east and passing to the right of Loch of Breck. At the road, turn left, ignore the left turn and continue on the quiet moorland road, to the head of Loch of Vadil. Here you may wish to pick up your outward route along the coast or continue on the road to a T-junction. Turn right to drop down the steepish hill into Walls.

Long-tailed ducks

Practicals

Type of walk: *Generally easy walking with two steady climbs. A very satisfactory walk along the peaceful coast and quiet roads of West Mainland.*

Distance: 6 miles/9.8km
Time: 3–4 hours
Maps: OS Explorer 467/Landranger 3

10

Huxter to Sandness Hill

Park in the car park at Huxter, grid ref 174573. Access this by driving towards West Mainland along the A971. Ignore the left turn to Walls and continue in the direction of Sandness. At the school do not take the continuing A-road, right to the pier, but drive along the narrow road ahead to its end at Huxter.

On the short diversion from the car park, before you start the walk, you reach a small ravine. Here there are **three watermills**, the upper two partially restored and the lowest completely. Go inside this to see the machinery. It is a click mill with a horizontal paddle wheel. Each thatched mill would have been shared by two or three families in the days when corn was grown.

Watermills, Huxter

Crowberry is found growing on moorland, wet peat bogs, among dry rocks on bare sand or on heath. Its short stem lies along the ground with its roots on the lower surface. The edges of its

Crowberry

37

leaves roll back and are about a third of an inch long. They are evergreen, smooth above and downy on the lower surface. They turn red when old. The minute flowers are purple-red and without stems. The edible fruits are about a third of an inch across and are usually black.

Walk 10

1 From the parking area follow the footpath, signed to the watermills, that soon swings left and continues to a stream. Here, in the small ravine, are the three watermills described above. Return to the parking area and turn right, south, to take a reinforced track heading over pasture, with the Loch of Huxter and the remains of a broch beside it. Carry on up the track to pass a burnt mound on the left.

2 At the track end head over the links to walk on along the cliffs. Across the Sound of Papa lies the hilly island of Papa Stour. Look with care over the cliff edge to see the magnificent folding and tilting of the sandstone and the volcanic lava that runs in bands through it. Climb a step-stile over the very long stone wall and stride on. Pass Loch of Skaaga on your left, then peer down the Hesti Geo. Walk the edge of the Bay of Deepdale steadily beginning to climb. Far down in the bay a series of stacks spike upwards. Climb up and up to Banks Head, from where there are spectacular views of the sheer cliffs sliding down to the bay.

3 Climb on. Now you are immensely high and everywhere that seemed high before is below you. As soon as you can spot below the great cleft of Deep Dale, strike inland, keeping to the right of the cairn on Ramma Vord, following the same contour to avoid losing height. Here you might see mountain hares, loping over the pasture. Go on, inland, to where you can spot a tall stone cairn high on Sandness Hill. Head towards it walking over heather, clubmoss, crowberry and lichen. Ascend over a 'sea' of shattered pink and blue stones to the cairn. To your left, in a hollow, lies a small loch,

Nether Shun. Walk on along the ridge to a stone shelter 810ft/246m and pause here to enjoy the fine view. Ahead lies another cairn and the trig point, 820ft/249m.

4 Return to the shelter. Drop down to the left side of the small loch and continue to descend over crowberry, heading towards a junction of walls below. As you go Scammi Dale lies to your right – keep well up the slope above it. When you have crossed the wall at the bottom of the hill, pick the driest way over the intervening wet area to cross a fence. Continue over the pasture. With a wall to your left, pass through the next gate to join the reinforced track taken earlier and follow it to Huxter.

Mountain Hare

Practicals

Type of walk: *Good walking. Steep climb to Banks Head. A challenging walk with great views over the jagged coastline and from the top of Sandness Hill.*

Distance:	4 miles/6.5km
Time:	3 hours
Maps:	OS Explorer 467/Landranger 3

11

Papa Stour

Park at West Burrafirth Pier, grid ref 257569.

To reach West Burrafirth pier and car ferry, leave the A971 at the second right turn, if travelling west, after Bixter. The signposted narrow road leads over wild moorland where birds nest along the verges. There is ample parking at the pier and good facilities. The car ferry takes you through the firth, past its islands, and then across the Sound of Papa, where you might spot porpoises. The distance is approximately one mile and the journey takes 35 minutes. Advanced booking is essential on 01957 722259. There is no shop, café or natural shelter from wind or rain on the island, but tea/coffee making facilities are available in the waiting room. Try to choose a good day and go well equipped. As you enter Housa Voe on your way to dock at the island's pier notice the dramatic red stacks guarding the way.

The largest stack is known as **The Maiden**. Legend says that a young girl, who had fallen in love with a low-born suitor, was confined to a stone house on top of the stack. She was rescued by her ardent lover and eventually he became an accepted member of the family.

The Vikings gave **Papa Stour** its name, which means the big island of priests. Celtic priests are believed to have lived here as early as the sixth century.

Soon after the start of your walk you pass **Gardie House**. Here, in the 19th century, Edwin Lindsay, an officer in the Indian army, was confined for 26 years by his father for refusing to fight a duel.

Porpoises

Walk 11

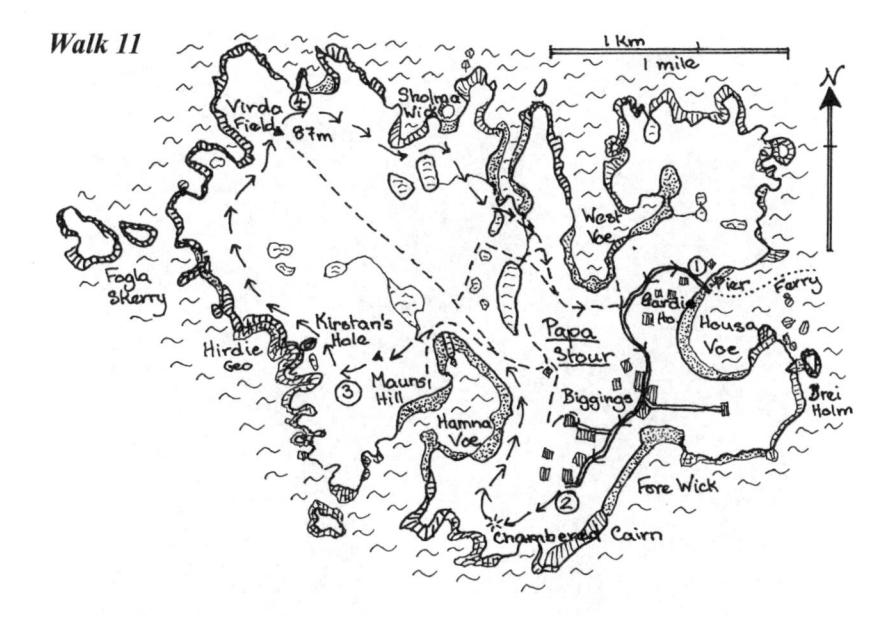

1. From the ferry walk up the hill to pass the ruins of Gardie House and continue along the road to Biggings where a stile gives access to excavations that revealed the foundations of a medieval Norse house. At the Kirk you might wish to go inside and enjoy the peace of the tiny church. Look for the fine stained glass window, a poignant memorial to those lost in the 1914–18 war. Stroll on to pass the old manse and then the village school. Opposite the latter take a footpath that leads to the foot of the Hill of Feilie (215ft/66m), passing the south end of the airstrip. Here, where only stones remain, was housed a leper colony. Nowadays it is believed that these outcasts didn't have leprosy but a disfiguring disease caused by a very poor diet.

2. Continue on the footpath to the top of the hill to see all that remains of a chambered cairn. Then walk a short way, south-east along the slope to see the waymarked remnants of a heel-shaped chambered cairn, a Neolithic burial site. Return by your outward route towards Biggins. Ignore the road, right, and go ahead to Mid Setter. Continue ahead and then on a wider track left to come close to the head of Hamma Voe. Stroll on around the northern head of the voe and continue to a small stream to look for two ruined watermills. Walk on to a fence. Do not cross it but walk beside it, on your left, along the slopes of Mauns Hill (130ft/40m). Continue ahead from the fence over the heath with a magnificent sea view ahead and bear right along the cliffs.

Kirstan's Hole, Papa Stour

3 As you continue, approach any of the geos, inlets, gloups, cliff edges with great care. Walk on to see Kirstan's's Hole – here a gloup has formed with a wide bridge of land intact between the great hole and the cliff edge. There is another gloup nearby; both are sheer and very deep and give little warning of their presence even on a bright sunny day. Continue on to pass above Hirdie Geo and pause to enjoy the natural arches, stacks and wonderful pink cliffs. Keep to the left of the large Loch of Aesha and head on over a boulder field to climb to the trig point (285ft/87m) in its walled shelter, on Virda Field.

4 Drop down the slope and begin to walk east along the indented coastline, past Sholma Wick and The Kiln, the latter a huge waterless hole with a rock arch. Press on keeping to the left of two small lochs, both of which supported watermills. Stroll on to pass on your left The Loch that Ebbs and Flows and go on to a gate in the fence.

Head right to a marker post where there is believed to have been a prehistoric settlement (3,000 BC). Close by are the remains of a crofthouse. Here pick up a clear causeway, heading east. This is one of the two 'meal' roads on the island. They were built by labour paid for with a meal during the famine in the 19th century. The meal road is soon lost under a track and this leads to a gate and a fence. Walk along the side of the fence to take a good stile to the road. Beyond, turn left and walk back to the pier.

Rabbit

Practicals

Type of walk: *Generally easy walking but strong shoes or boots advisable. Choose good weather for a wonderful day of exploration of this magic island. Otters frequent the voes.*

Distance: 7–8 miles/12–13km
Time: 8 hours
Maps: OS Explorer 467 (essential)/Landranger 3

12

Vementry

Park in the layby on your right, just before a cattle grid, beside the northern loch of the two Lochs of Hostigates, grid ref 312596. To access this, leave Lerwick by the A970 and then take the A971 to Bixter, where you turn right onto the B9071 for Aith. Bear left to continue along the west side of Aith Voe, through the peninsula of Aith Ness. Drive almost to the end of the road and the layby.

The two track man-made **causeway** crosses The Brigs. There is an island half-way and a gate. Depending on the tide, the causeway will cross either an outlet from the fresh-water loch or an inlet from the sea loch. During the equinoctial spring tides and westerly gales it is inundated with water.

Causeway, The Brigs (at high tide)

Walk 12

1. Take the good track, signed 'Path to Clousta', going off south, left, beyond a metal gate. Enjoy the delightful way as it passes through heather above the other Loch of Hostigates. Here you might spot a mountain hare, loping through the low vegetation. Pass two small lochans. Follow the gently ascending path to the brow of the hill and beyond you can see the large Loch of Clousta with its several green-topped islands. Go on downhill through the schist and heather to cross The Brigs, an extension of North Voe of Clousta. Stride the causeway.

2. Continue ahead uphill. There is no path but the route is marked by tall waymark posts. On reaching the brow you can see settlement of Clousta below, clustered around the head of the Voe of Clousta. Begin the steady descent following the waymarks to join a farm track. Walk in front of a cottage and turn left down an access track to the road by the shore.

3. Turn right, signed 'Coastal Walk'. After a few yards, bear left to walk the shallow cliffs of the beautiful, indented coastline of the Ness of Clousta. Look for mergansers on the Voe to your left. Continue past a ruined wall, plantiecrub and sheep

Red-breasted Mergansers

pund. Then as you round the next corner, you have a spectacular view of the dramatic cliffs of Neeans Neap. Look across the Voe to the north side of the last two houses to see a small promontory on which stands a ruined broch.

4   Stroll on round the final promontory of the Ness and continue with North Voe to your left. Pass more plantiecrubs and the remains of an earlier settlement. Go on towards The Brigs, walking over sundew in the wetter areas. Here you might spot an otter. Re-cross the causeway and begin the lovely walk back, through the heather to rejoin your car.

Lady's Smock (Milkmaids)

Otter

Practicals

Type of walk: *Easy walking. A delightful route through heather on a good path followed by an excellent coastal walk.*

Distance: 4½ miles/7.4km
Time: 2–3 hours
Maps: OS Explorer 467/Landranger 3

13

Muckle Roe

Park on Muckle Roe at grid ref 322628. Access this by the A970 from Lerwick to Brae. Continue left round the head of Busta Voe to take the first left, signed Muckle Roe. Go over the bridge and bear left to drive on along the road to its end where there is space for parking just beyond.

On a fast-flowing burn, a short way upstream from a ruined croft-house or a small township, you might find the ruins of one or more **horizontal watermills**. The fast flowing water was channelled into the lower part of the housing to a wheel with blades. These drove the millstones that ground the barley or wheat.

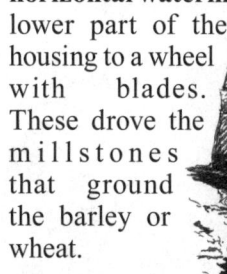

Watermill, North Ham, Muckle Roe

1 Walk the wide gated track, which climbs steadily north-east, ignoring a left turn. Keep ahead, avoiding the next left turn and continue through the valley between Muckla Field and Mid Field. The track has been cut through red granite which is heavily overlaid with peat on which heather flourishes. Press on along the sheltered way, which cuts deep

47

into the moorland heart of this little island. Here on the top of the ling on the bank above, you might spot a plump bullet-headed golden plover.

Walk 13

2 Carry on past Burki Waters then cross a small burn issuing from the loch, which accompanies you to your left. Look ahead for a first glorious view of Town Loch at North Ham, the valley opening out into a wide flat grassy area. Where the track swings left and crosses the burn, walk ahead to a gate and bear right on the footpath to pass in front of an old dwelling, crossing its once extensive grazing land. Keep to the right side of the lovely Town Loch until you reach a gate. Do not pass through but climb the slope to come to the side of a watermill. Enjoy this secret hollow where the burn, which has tumbled out of Mill Loch, descends in many pretty falls. It is this stream that was diverted to turn the millstones.

Golden Plovers

3 Return to the gate and pass through. Continue beside the fence to your right to pass below the steep-sided gill, through which the burn continues to join Town Loch. Stroll on to the lovely bay of North Ham and here do some summer dreaming. The glorious deep blue inlet is edged with huge red cliffs, stacks and a natural arch. Green and orange lichen thrive on the red granite and the colour combination is quite beautiful. Cross the footbridge or the bank of rounded boulders that separates the loch from the sea, and bear left to pass below the end of a fence. Then begin

to ascend the ridge ahead from where the dramatic coastline is revealed. Enjoy its many inlets, geos and stacks but proceed with care. Look for mats of moss campion ranging in colour from pale lilac to deep pink.

Moss Campion

4 Descend the slope to the side of South Ham, where the sand is a warm red gold. Climb the fence and walk on. Cross the end of the track you walked earlier and take the gate on your right. Pass another ruined crofthouse as you cut across the Strom Ness promontory, taking care as you round the side of immensely deep Geo of Strom Ness. From here strike up, gently, onto the rocky top of the West Hill of Ham from where you can see Papa Stour and, in the misty distance, the high cliffs of Foula.

5 Keep well to the left of Dandi Geo to come to several small lochs. From the nearest one a burn issues in a great fall to the foot of a deep ravine. Continue ahead between the two nearest lochs. Walk over the rough grass and shattered rock passing between the warm pink outcrops. Carry on keeping left of Muckla Water. When you reach the foot of Gilsa Water, follow a narrow, safe path along the side of the loch. Climb the slope at the other end and continue beside Loch of Brunthill. Then the narrow path stretches ahead through heather.

6 Soon a lovely bay lies far below, its rich red-gold sand turning the water turquoise and then purple. Just when you feel the way is becoming too 'white knuckle', the path is protected by a handrail and you can enjoy the magic scene below. Continue to a fence, which you cross by a stile. Dawdle on along the distinct path, above another glorious sandy bay. At a small cairn begin the descent of the heather cliff to step across a stream and then a track. Walk the footpath as it continues beyond the track and follow it to join the track taken at the outset of your walk. Go through the gate to rejoin your vehicle just beyond.

Practicals

Type of walk: *Easy walking. One of the loveliest walks on Shetland – on a good day.*

Distance: 6½ miles/10.6km
Time: 4–5 hours
Maps: OS Explorer 469/Landranger 3

14

Ness of Hillswick

Park in the settlement of Hillswick close to the toilet block, grid ref 283771.

To access this, take the west branch of the A970 to the village.

The walk round the **Ness of Hillswick** is magnificent. It starts and ends gently, but towards the headland the cliffs are high, sheer and glorious. It is easy walking all the way but there are many dangerous edges, hidden until the last moment, so be wary – especially if walking with children. Dogs not allowed.

Gordi stack and the The Drongs, Hillswick

1. Walk on to the end of the road to pass through a gate on the left, opposite The Smithy to continue along the shallow cliffs, where in spring the turf is sprinkled with wild flowers. At Tur Ness the sea has undermined the jagged rocks of the cliff edge and created a clear pool through which you can see the large coloured cobbles on its bed. Stroll on with care as the cliffs become higher and the path steeper. Fulmars and kittiwakes nest on the ledges of the rock gardens. Look for a natural arch as you go and watch out for otters that have left evidence of their presence.

Kittiwakes

2. Cross the fence and walk on the lovely way to reach a small stone ruin close to a burn. Follow the stream inland to see a ruined watermill and then continue on to just before the Loch of Niddister to see the remains of a prehistoric cairn or burial place. Walk on round the loch to a small promontory where there is evidence of a burnt mound. Then return to the shore and carry on. At the Bight of Niddister concrete steps descend the shallow rocks from which, once, boats set off with supplies for the lighthouse at Baa Taing.

3. Begin the steady climb up the cliffs. Look for spectacularly layered rock formations that tilt vertically to the shore. Go on round the Queen Geos, where

Walk 14

some rocks take on a diadem shape. Stroll the narrow path around the glorious headland, always prepared for it to end suddenly in a sheer drop. Follow the white and black posts, which lead you safely to the lighthouse from where you can see over St Magnus Bay to Papa Stour and Foula. Go on around the headland where, between Gordi Stack and Windy Geo, you have a fine view of the fantastically shaped Drongs: weird-shaped pink granite stacks.

4 Cross the fence and then continue on to view the flower-topped Isle of Westerhouse from the Pund of Grevasand, where great care should be exercised. Descend steadily along the cliffs and then ascend to the highest point of your walk, 269ft/82m of cliff. Descend again to Ber Dale, from where the wonderful red granite cliffs, the Heads of Grocken, welcome you across the bay of Sand Wick.

5 Keep to the outside of the fence and stroll the low cliffs to join a track. This continues to the left of a sturdy wall. Follow it a little way round Sand Wick, close to a stretch of golden sand edged with pebbles, and then take a narrow path behind the beach that leads to another track. This runs along the far side of an oval-shaped cemetery, where once stood a medieval chapel. Look for 18th century headstones built into the wall on either side of the gate. Walk into the village, where you might like to visit St Magnus Church, built in 1870.

Silverweed

Practicals

Type of walk: *A marvellous walk with much to see. Easy walking but go with care.*

Distance:	4½miles/7.4km
Time:	2–3 hours
Maps:	OS Explorer 469/Landranger 3

15

Eshaness Lighthouse

Park at Eshaness Lighthouse, grid ref 206785. To access this take the A970 north and drive through Mavis Grind, a thin strip of land with the North Sea to the north-east and the Atlantic to the west. Where the A970 divides, take the western branch, left, and wind round the Ura Firth. At grid ref 291778, turn right onto the B9078 and continue to West Loch to take the signposted right turn for the lighthouse.

In the middle of the cemetery of the site of Cross Kirk medieval church, stands the tomb of **Donald Robertson**. He died in 1848, aged 63. Legend tells that he was mistakenly given nitre instead of Epsom salts for an un-named malady. He died within five hours. Laurance Tulloch of Clothister, who made the mistake, rapidly left the district and set up shop in 1852 in Aberdeen.

Holes of Scraada, Eshaness

1 Walk north, right, over the closely-cropped turf, colourful with low-growing thrift in late spring. Approach with care the edge of Calder's Geo, which is immensely deep, dark and extensive. You can see a cave far below, which is really a subterranean passage that links with the sea on the north side. Stroll on north, keeping on the seaward side of several small lochs, Lochs of Dridgeo. Go over the wall by a sturdy stile and walk round another huge geo. Carry on to view the rugged Moo Stack, which is lichen-covered and has a natural arch. Climb a small slope to look down on the tortured rocks of Scraada.

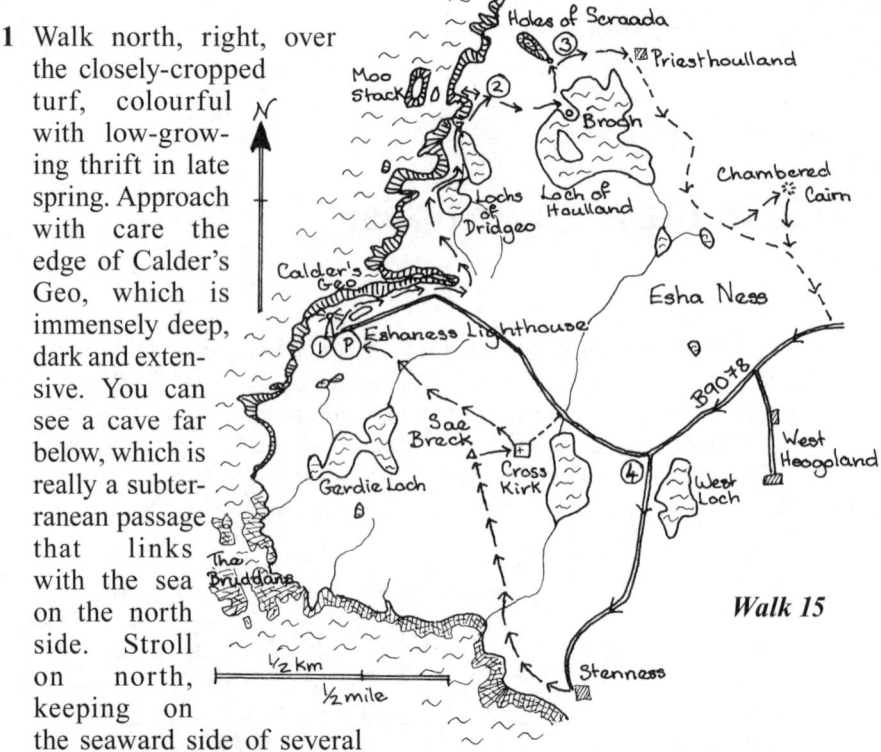

2 Return to the wall, do not cross but continue down beside it to the Loch of Houlland, on which stands a ruined broch, dating from the third century to the first century BC. Climb through the outer wide stone ramparts guarding access from the shore. Step into the central hollow, where the walls, in parts, are 12ft high. Walk along the small stream that flows out of the loch. It once powered several watermills. Beyond is the dramatic blowhole known as the Holes of Scraada, where the natural rock vault of subterranean caves has collapsed, and into it the little burn tumbles. Be wary as you approach. The hole is very deep. It is connected to the sea by a passage, 110yds long.

3 Walk on around the Loch of Houlland heading towards a crofthouse, Priesthoulland. When level with the house bear right along a wide grassy track to a gate. Beyond, turn right to walk a reinforced track that takes you through heather moorland – the territory of curlew,

oystercatcher, wheatear and arctic tern. Stroll on until you are level with a lochan, to your right, then strike left to the top of a small hill to see March Cairn, a square-chambered cairn composed of large boulders. It once stood four feet tall. Return to the track and walk on to join a road, where you turn right to continue. To the far left look for The Drongs and, nearer, Dore Holm with its huge natural arch through which a boat can pass.

Oystercatchers

4   Ignore the road to the lighthouse and continue to the end of the road at Stenness. The settlement was once a fishing station, ideally sited being sheltered by the Isle of Stenness and the Skerry of Eshaness. Go through the gate on the right at the end of the road and return along the shallow cliffs. Cross the fence and walk beside the wall to its end. Pass through a gate and strike up towards the trig point on the top of Sae Breck from where there is a magnificent view. Drop down the hill slope to visit the immaculately tended site of Cross Kirk, a medieval church. Here in the middle is the tomb of Donald Robertson. Johnny Notions (see Walk 16) is also buried here. Leave the cemetery and climb the slope of the hill to where you can follow the telegraph wires across the sward towards the lighthouse and the parking area. Or join the road, walked earlier, and turn left and left again.

Marsh Marigold (Kingcup)

Practicals

Type of Walk: *A dramatic walk with lots of interest along the way.*

Distance: 4miles/6.5km
Time: 3–4 hours
Maps: OS Explorer 469/Landranger 3

16

Hamnavoe

Park in a layby on the right, grid ref 243806, just beyond two large standing stones, on the right, almost at the end of the single track road to the settlement of Hamnavoe. Access this by, first, taking the same route, as for Walk 15. At Braewick turn right following the signpost directions for Hamnavoe.

Johnny Notions, whose real name was John Williamson, was born in the middle of the 18th century. He developed a method of inoculation against smallpox, which had devastated Shetland throughout the 18th century. None of his patients ever became a victim. He is buried in Cross Kirk cemetery (see Walk 15).

The Giant's Stone, Hamnavoe

1. Walk back from the parking area for a short way past the standing stones to take, now on the left, an easy-to-walk two-mile-long way, reinforced with fine red sandstone, winding pleasingly through the heather of Grind Hill. Continue past Mill Lochs, then Craagles Water and on to go through a gate in a sturdy wall. Ahead in the distance lies the crofthouse of Tingon, surrounded by green pastures. Carry on until you reach the Burn of Tingon.

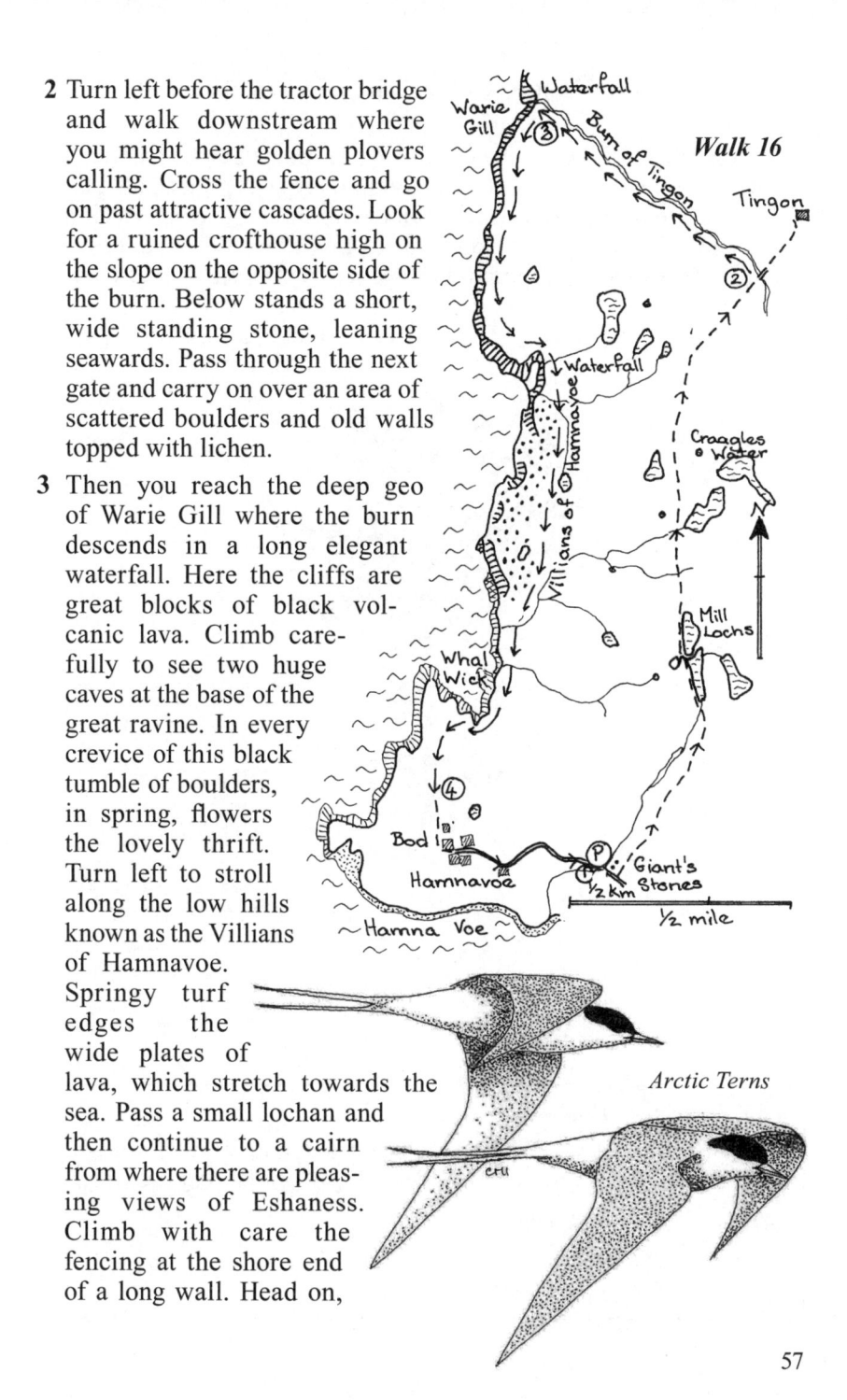

2 Turn left before the tractor bridge and walk downstream where you might hear golden plovers calling. Cross the fence and go on past attractive cascades. Look for a ruined crofthouse high on the slope on the opposite side of the burn. Below stands a short, wide standing stone, leaning seawards. Pass through the next gate and carry on over an area of scattered boulders and old walls topped with lichen.

3 Then you reach the deep geo of Warie Gill where the burn descends in a long elegant waterfall. Here the cliffs are great blocks of black volcanic lava. Climb carefully to see two huge caves at the base of the great ravine. In every crevice of this black tumble of boulders, in spring, flowers the lovely thrift. Turn left to stroll along the low hills known as the Villians of Hamnavoe. Springy turf edges the wide plates of lava, which stretch towards the sea. Pass a small lochan and then continue to a cairn from where there are pleasing views of Eshaness. Climb with care the fencing at the shore end of a long wall. Head on,

Walk 16

Arctic Terns

following a row of fence posts, which lead you across small streams to a fence.

4 Beyond stroll left across the pasture to pass a small lochan where, late spring arctic terns nest between marsh marigolds on a small island. Continue to a gate to a track and follow this round to come to Johnny Notions' House, now a camping bod. Join the metalled road, turn left and walk down and then uphill to rejoin your vehicle by the standing stones.

Roseroot

Practicals

Type of walk: *Easy and interesting. Can be boggy in parts after rain. The sudden approach to the black cliffs can be very exciting.*

Distance: 4½ miles/7.4km
Time: 2–3 hours
Maps: OS Explorer 469/Landranger 3

17

Ronas Hill

Park at Collafirth Hill, grid ref 335835. Access this by the reinforced 1½ mile track, constructed by the Ministry of Defence, which leads off west from the A970, at grid ref 354836. From the parking area in front of the gate to the disused radio station you have a distant, enticing view of the cairn on Ronas Hill and, south-west, of The Drongs.

There are no footpaths over **Roga Field**, **Mid Field** or **Ronas Hill**. Right from the start of the walk much of the ground supports flattish, low boulders, easy to step on and balance. Between the majority of boulders are soft mounds of woolly hair moss, heather and a variety of other plants more likely to found in the Arctic such as mountain azalea. Peaty patches and fine gravel broken off from the rocks, over time, can also be seen. This vast area makes for easy walking, stepping from boulder to boulder or plant mounds to plant mounds.

Chambered Cairn, Ronas Hill

A few yards west of the trig point stands a well-preserved **single chambered cairn**, with the entrance on the eastern end. Some walkers, with a torch, will want to crawl inside, others to peer inside to see a passageway leading to a four feet high chamber composed of huge blocks. Originally the cairn measured about 50ft high. The trig point is surrounded by a walled shelter, and provides welcome protection from unfriendly weather.

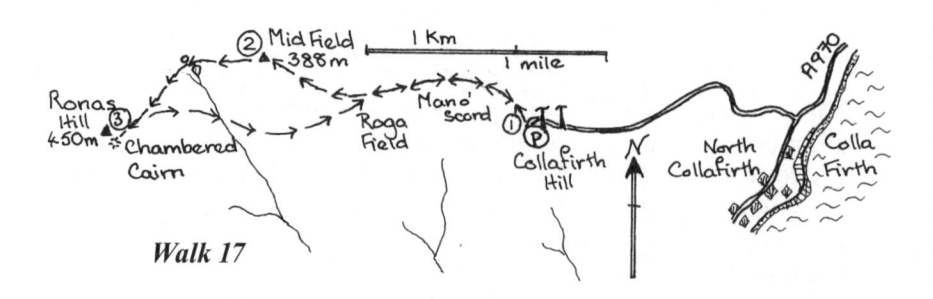

Walk 17

1. From the parking area, descend the slope bearing slightly right, north-west, in the direction of a cairn on Man O'Scord. Avoid wet areas, though after a period of dry weather it is possible to use convenient stones to make an easy crossing. Then begin your ascent, west, of Mid Field, 1266ft/388m, keeping to the right of the cairn on Roga Field. The top is more grassy than stone-clad. From the top you have a good view of Ronas Hill cairn and the direction, slightly west, in which to continue.

2. Descend the slope to the pass through a wettish area between two small lochans, where you might put up snipe, to start your ascent to the summit. It is steep at first and then lessening until you reach the magic top. The views are astounding. Look for Fair Isle, south, and Muckle Flugga Lighthouse, north.

   Snipe

3. Descend from the top in the same direction as you went up. At the foot, pass between the lochans and then wind right, keeping well above the large wet patches about the Grud Burn. Remain at the same height as you contour round, with the Collafirth radio station in view,

below the cairn on Mid Field and keeping above an area of peat hags. Continue ahead to reach the cairn on Man O'Scord and then head up the slope to the parking area.

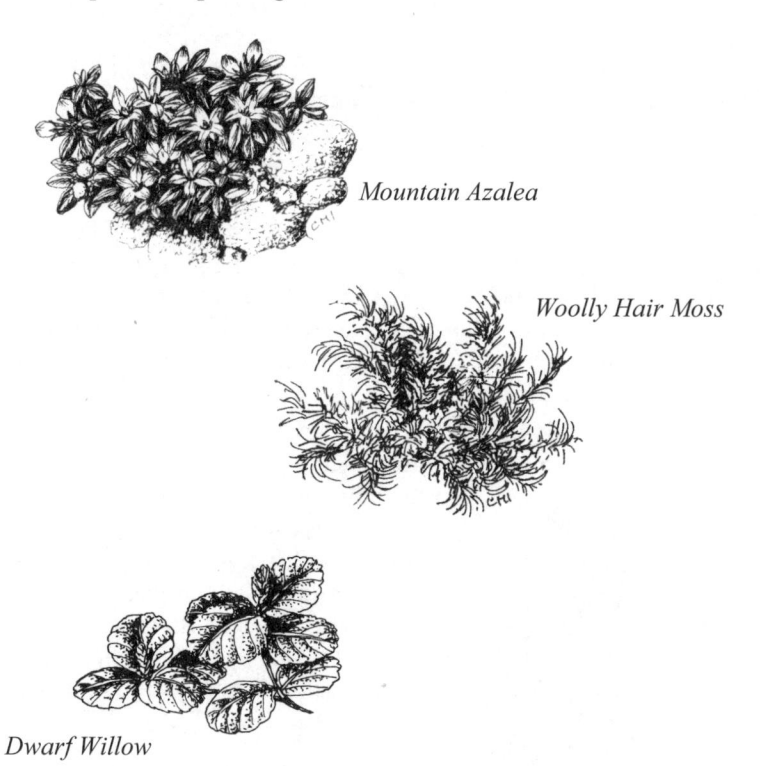

Mountain Azalea

Woolly Hair Moss

Dwarf Willow

Practicals

Type of walk: *A steady climb for almost all the way to the top over unexpectedly easy ground. Remember the winds can be strong and icy, the tops covered in mist and it attracts the worst of the rain-bearing clouds. It is fairly featureless ground, so not a good walk in mist. Take a compass. Choose a good day to get the greatest enjoyment.*

Distance: 4½ miles/7.4km
Time: 4 hours
Maps: OS Explorer469/Landranger 3

18

North Roe, North Mainland

Park in North Roe, grid ref 366899. Access village by the A970 into North Mainland, pass below the red hills, the Beorgs of Skelberry, and continue to the striking village. Go past the school on the left and then the church on the right to park on a hard-standing area where the road to Sandvoe goes left.

The Beorgs of Uyea Axe Factory lies three miles along a distinct but rough track. Here, in a hollow, roofed with granite slabs, ancient man obtained pieces of speckled felsite rock, sharp enough to be used for cutting, producing the famous Shetland knife which was used all over the islands. Bracken and moss grow inside his factory now. Around the site lie piles of waste – unique blue stone, speckled as

Cairn and Neolithic spoil heap, Beorgs of Uyea

if hailstones had rained down, patterning the rock with symmetrical spots. Many of the Neolithic products can be seen in the Shetland Museum. Please do not take any samples from this magical site.

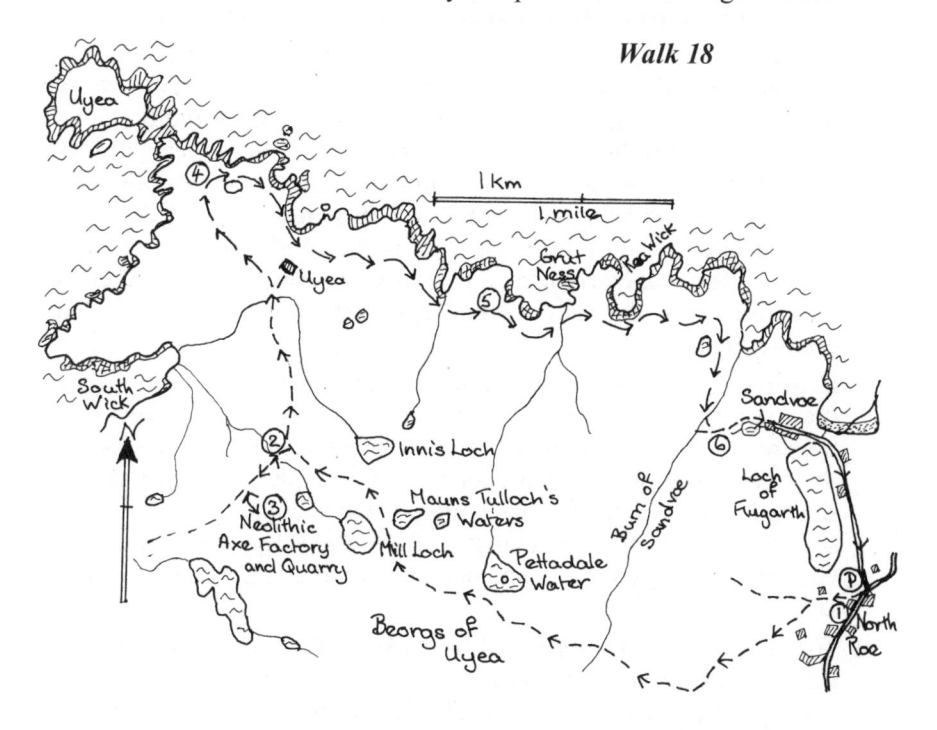

Walk 18

1 Walk back a few steps along the road to take the track, right, that goes off in front of a hut used by the coastguard service. At the Y-junction of tracks, bear left to stride on beside Vatsendi Burn to your right. The way makes for stark walking, as if the last glacier had only just passed through. Grey boulders lie scattered through the heather. Keep to the main track as it swings right and passes through a gate. Go past sheep pens and ford a burn. Follow the wide track, a masterly piece of excavation through ten feet of peat in some places. It comes near to Pettadale Water and below the forbidding slopes of the Beorgs of

Red-throated Divers

Uyea. Then the gated way passes between Mill Loch and Mauns Tulloch's Waters where you might spot red-throated divers. Each time the way appears to branch, keep to the right fork, until you can see the coast in the distance.

2   After three miles take a good left branch swinging down through the heather and over a burn. Look left, as the track starts to climb, to see a tall cairn on the skyline, with stripes of shattered blue rock around it. Climb the track to a wide bend, cross the fence and walk over heather across a valley and up over a one- stone-high wall to the cairn. This is where the stone was quarried – a Neolithic spoil heap. There are stone-lined hollows in the spoil, probably remains of huts. From the cairn, walk on south-east to locate the axe factory. Look for a boulder with a small cairn on it. This marks the 12ft granite block shelter.

3   Return over the heather to the good track and descend right to join the main track once more. Turn left and stroll for nearly a mile towards the crofthouse of Uyea. At the end of the track, walk on to the Ness and look across (depending on the tides) a spit of sand or sea to the grassy isle of Uyea, which is rich in copper. (People trying to cross the sand have been cut off by the tide – so be warned.) Grazing is good on the island and sheep are driven across the sand at low tide.

4   Turn east, right, to walk round North Wick Bay, where you pass the remains of several fishing huts. Follow the fence around the Breck and continue to join a distinct track. This leads to the ruins of Brevligarth, with its magnificent views of Stacks, jutting skywards like jagged black teeth. The cliffs, which receive the full force of the wind, are denuded of vegetation and the rock is weathered into tortured shapes. Stroll on with care around several very steep geos, colourful with large clumps of yellow roseroot. Continue over the lower slopes of North Hill and then descend the other side to cross a burn. In the next bay look for horizontal pink granite, intruding into grey vertical layers of lava.

5   Continue over the short turf and then clamber over an enormous boulder field that stretches to the cliff edge of Grut Ness. Walk on round Raa Wick and then, maintaining height, follow the contours round the slopes to Heoga Neap. From here you can see Ronas Hill. Stroll on round the dramatic headland, then descend steadily to the tiny pebble shore, Roer Mill, far below, at the foot of the Burn of Sandvoe. Walk inland, upstream, passing the foundations of some dwellings to join the end of a track and walk east.

6 Go past a small loch and continue to the tiny hamlet of Sandvoe. Carry on along the metalled road, with the lovely sandy bay to your left and the Loch of Flugarth to your right. Pass the cemetery and press on for half a mile to the A-road and your vehicle.

Spring Squill

Practicals

Type of walk: *The track at the start is long and sometimes rough underfoot. The return over the cliffs is good roller-coaster hill walking. It is a challenging walk and all the usual precautions should be taken.*

Distance: 8–9 miles/14–15km
Time: 5 hours
Maps: OS Explorer 469/Landranger 1

19

Isbister to the Point of Fethaland

Park on the right just before a gate, leaving room for turning vehicles, grid ref 372909. Access this by driving through Mavis Grind and then, eventually, taking the northern branch of A970. Continue in the direction of North Roe and then Isbister where the road ends at the gate. Beyond, walkers have access. Dogs are prohibited.

The Isle of Fethaland, an unbelievably beautiful hilly place of green pastures and dramatic seascapes, is the most northerly point on Shetland's North Mainland. As you walk, remember the children who, as late as the early 1940s, trekked daily the then almost trackless two miles, each way, between their homes and school.

The isle is linked to Fethaland by a wonderful **spit of boulders and pebbles**. It is a tenth of a mile in width and is approached by greensward. It separates the Atlantic from Yell Sound and, on a good day, with the wind in the right direction, the rollers come crashing in on one side while gentle turquoise waves lap the other. To the left of the spit, a huge embankment of great boulders, ten feet high, has been thrown up. Below them you might see grey seals bob.

Ruined fishing lodges, Fethaland

1. Pass through the gate and follow the good track, signposted 'Path to Fethaland' as it swings north, uphill. This is a breezy high-level way through sheep pasture, with occasional glimpses of sea and loch through the rolling hills. Continue on the gated way and as you climb the hill, nothing prepares you for the magnificent view towards the Isle of Fethaland, a hilly up-tilting green headland that leans dramatically towards you – and hides more glory beyond. Continue on, keeping right of the Upper Loch of Setter and then the Loch of Breibister. Follow the way as it goes on past the Rigg of Breibister and then on to the spit of land that links the isle to the mainland.

2. On the spit stand a dozen or more ruined fishing lodges, once used by deep-sea fishermen between early June and the middle of August. Today these roofless, heavily lichened picturesque dwellings belie the noise and bustle of a once-busy station. Only the waves, the oystercatchers and the fulmars break the silence. Continue over the boulder spit and once on the island, pass through the wall and ascend the grassy path ahead. Walk with care along sheer west cliffs to see jagged Yellow Stack close to the squat white lighthouse. Beyond, the high land narrows and drops to The Point of Fethaland, where spring squill covers the grass like blue snow. Pause here and look out to see the massive Ramna Stacks, an RSPB reserve.

3. Turn south and walk back along the east coast of the island to pass several geos including Cleber Geo. Here, look for a large rock face of soapstone, once much quarried for bowls and pots. It is much carved with ancient graffiti. Cross the spit and begin your return, left, along the east coast of Fethaland. Pass round the wide Wick of Breibister, below a ruined croft and watermill. Dawdle across Lanyar Taing and then on to pass an old sheep enclosure. On the slopes above, a huge rock of quartz catches the sunlight. Walk with care along the edge of the very deep Eislin Geo.

Walk 19

67

4 Climb the next two fences and continue over the flower-spangled pasture, past another great sea bight into this eastern coast. Approach circumspectly an overhanging crag, split down the middle, with a cave below. Negotiate the third fence and then drop down to cross a hollow, through which runs a small burn and where considerable drainage has been done. Pass the remains of more sheep enclosures. Just beyond, and before the next fence, look left and out onto Lokati Kame, the flat top of which appears to be a stack. In fact it is joined, at its base, by a knife-edge of rock. Here, you can see, from afar, the grass-covered foundations of a possible Celtic monastery. Do **not** cross the knife-edge of rock. In Walk 20 a similar site is seen, on the Birrier on Yell.

Grey Seal

Kidney vetch

5 Cross the next fence and take care as you round two high, huge, grassy hollows that slope steeply down to small stony beaches. Overlooking and ahead of the second is the towering Head of Virdibreck. Go on to climb to the top of the Head to see another monastic site by looking northward across the beach, far below, to a rocky promontory topped by green sward that slopes towards the sea. It is visible only from the top of the Head. The promontory is known as the Kame of Isbister. On the green sward you can see the grassy outlines of the walls of four or five buildings.

6 Return to the foot of the Head and bear left to walk beside the Loch of Houllsquey. Cross the fence, on your right, at the end of the loch and walk its south shore to join a good track. Follow this as it descends, left, steadily towards Isbister where you might like to visit the cemetery of St Magnus, which has interesting gravestones made of wood. Continue along the track to rejoin your vehicle.

Practicals

Type of walk: *A challenging walk with much to see. It should not be missed.*

Distance:	6–7 miles/10–11km
Time:	4 hours
Maps:	OS Explorer 459/Landranger 1

20

West Sandwick, Yell

Park on the Island of Yell, near Sandwick, grid ref 454895. To access this leave Ulsta, South Yell, by the A968 and drive for six miles to take the third turn on the left signed for West Sandwick and Hjarkland. Descend for a tenth of a mile and park in a layby at the side of the turn for Hjarkland. To reach Ulsta on the Island of Yell take the ferry from Toft on the north-east coast of Mainland. Ferries run regularly and the crossing takes approximately 20 minutes.

Yell is the second largest island in Shetland after Mainland. It is 19 miles in length and has a maximum breadth of 7½ miles. Its bedrock is mainly composed of schist. A blanket of peat, sometimes 10ft

The Birrier, Yell

thick covers much of its interior. The island has been inhabited since Neolithic times and several brochs have been identified.

The Birrier promontory slopes quite steeply towards the sea. A very narrow ridge connects it to the mainland. A derelict wall on the landward side of the promontory encloses the green sward, where there are traces of buildings which might have been part of a monastic settlement. These resemble the Kame of Isbister immediately opposite over the Sound of Yell. The approach to the promontory is seriously dangerous and walkers should not attempt to cross the connecting fragile ridge.

1 Stride down the unclassified road to West Sandwick, with the Loch of Scattlands to your left. Just beyond, turn right to take a signed reinforced track. A short way along bear right and then wind left through a car park and on along a path and steps, down to the lovely sandy West Sandwick Bay. Walk left, cross a fence and wander along the shallow cliff. As you continue look for a low natural arch where the deep blue water of the sea turns to green. Climb the wooden bars at the seaward end of a fence to reach the point opposite the Brough, a tiny tidal island, where stands the remains of a broch. Cross a tiny pebble beach, which could be difficult at very high tides. Then scramble up the stepped gneiss rock face to the broch, which has an outer rampart on the north side. The view from here is superb.

2 Return the same way to the sandy beach and step across a narrow burn, climb the shallow cliff and go north along the seaward side of the fence. Cross two fences and continue on to wind round Punds Geo, where schist is laid in vertical sheets. Press on ahead to cross the burn that flows out of Mill Loch and look upstream to see a watermill, with its paddles and millstone. Then ascend

The Head (185ft/56m) from where you have a first view of the Loch of Birriesgirt.

3 Descend gently to the side of burn that leaves the loch and tumbles in three graceful waterfalls before reaching the sea. Stroll on to walk beside the fence, keeping it to your left. Ascend, steadily ahead, towards the dramatic cliff-girt promontory of Birrier. Continue until you can see the oddly-shaped pinnacle of rock, aptly named The Old Wife of Birrier. Beyond the pinnacle, on the flat-topped continuation of the jutting promontory, it is thought that there might have been a monastic settlement, similar to that seen on the Kame of Isbister (walk 19) which it faces across Yell Sound.

4 To return, strike inland for 50 yards and then descend to Loch Birriesgirt passed earlier. On the way look for a circle of rocks, with a scattering of stones of various sizes which is believed to be a burnt mound. Stroll along the east side of the quiet sheet of water. Beyond the fence, keep on past the loch steadily ascending slightly left over heather moorland with much peat. Look back for a grand view of the Birrier and its Old Wife. As you breast a small rise, look ahead to see a track passing through the heather to the skyline. You should aim to join it just above Mill Loch. Stride on along the track for nearly a mile, ignoring two tracks that lead off right. Then follow it as it bears left to join the road, along which you walk to join your vehicle.

Purple Sandpiper

Practicals

Type of walk: *This is a pleasing walk, sometimes challenging, over remote countryside. Could be wet between the two lochs. Choose a good day and don't forget to take your map with you.*

Distance: 7 miles/11.4km
Time: 4 hours
Maps: OS Explorer 470/Landranger 1

21a

Gloup, North Yell

Park in the small grassy area below the fishermen's memorial, grid ref 506045. Access this by the A968, B9082 and the B9083. Continue ahead when the latter turns right to Breckon. Then, after 1¼ miles, where the road turns sharp right, look for the sign to the memorial, on the left. Drive up the track to the parking area.

Gloup was the second largest fishing station in Shetland when open boats with square sails, oars and crewed by six men, were in use. Fifty-eight fishermen perished when a great storm arose while they were deep-sea fishing in July 1881. The names of the boats and the crew and where they lived, are listed on the memorial.

Above the list on the **memoria**l is a carved statue of a **woman and child**, the woman with her hand shading her eyes as she peers out to sea. The woman and child represent the many widows and fatherless children left after the tragedy. The woman has a beautiful face. The memorial was erected in 1981.

Fishermen's Memorial, Gloup

1 Walk through the gate to the sad memorial where you will want to pause. Then go back through the gate and take the small gate, on the left, out of the car park and walk left beside the wall on the left with the dramatic Gloup Voe far down to the right. Beyond the gate

in the fence climb steadily left to join a track. As you ascend you have a bird's-eye view of the inlet deep in its ravine of gneiss and of the wild moorland around. Follow the track as it climbs to the trig point on the hill, Scordaback, (373ft/113m). The highest point (376ft/114m) lies a little further ahead. Here you may see a merlin the only bird of prey to occur regularly on Shetland.

Walk 21a

2 Then press on, descending until you are level with the Mare's Pool below, but still well up the slopes, at the head of the Voe. From here you may wish to descend quite steeply almost to the shore of the Pool and return along a narrow path just above the water. Or you may prefer to return by your outward route for a glorious view of the coast, which gets better with every step you take.

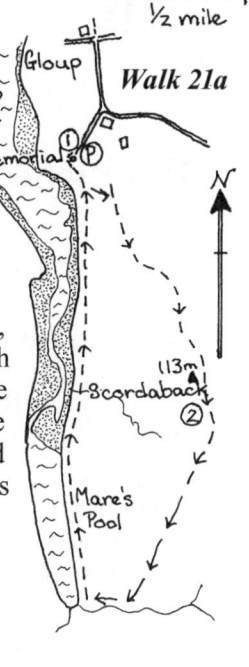

Merlin

Practicals

Type of walk: *A dramatic walk over the top. Take care along the side of the Voe.*

Distance: 2 miles/3.4km
Time: 2 hours
Maps: Explorer 470/Landranger 1

21b

Breakon, Yell

Park at the end of the road in a small parking area just before the outbuildings of the farm at Breakon, grid ref 526045. Access this by the A968, B9082, B9083 then turn right at the signpost for the Sands of Breakon.

In the centre of the cemetery stands all that remains of the **church of St Olaf,** Kirk of Ness, which served North Yell until the middle of the 18th century. Wander around the gravestones and read the personal tragedies inscribed on some of them. A sturdy wall encloses the graveyard.

In the sand dunes there is much **evidence of earlier occupation by man** but this is mainly lost under the ever shifting sand which can envelope everything and then uncover it again depending on the prevailing wind and storm damage. Understanding of the archaeological time-scale is apparently almost impossible because the evidence gets in the wrong place.

St. Olaf's Church, Breakon

1. Take the signed gate on the other side of the road from the car park and follow the path down towards a stream. To visit the beach turn left beyond the first fence. Go through a gate and down railed steps to the sand.

Walk 21b

Alternatively go ahead to cross the stream by a bridge, go over a stile and walk the path behind the dunes. Carry on where marram grass binds the sand on either side. To your left lies the glorious shell-sand beach, part of a dune system which because of the wind and wave action is constantly changing. If the weather is good, you could linger a long time here. Then take the ladderstile at the west end of the wall, or the gate on the right (east) to walk on along the grassy headland, Ness of Houlland, which shelters the glorious sands from the north-easterly winds. Do not continue on to Outsta Ness, made dangerous by storm damage.

2   Or you might prefer to cut across the landward end of the Ness to spend time looking for evidence of early settlers. Carry on along the magnificent coastline where fulmars, kittiwakes and ravens nest and on round the spectacular Brei Wick with a grand view across to Unst. Head on until you come to Kirk Loch. Cross the exit stream close to the lovely sandy stretch of water and walk uphill. Go over a fence by a ruined crofthouse and head for a track marked by orange floats (balloon-like waymarks). Turn left at the end to visit the cemetery, which lies west of the loch.

3   Return around the loch and climb the slope. Descend the other side and continue across the pastures to the prominent broch, dating between 100 BC and AD 200, on the cliff edge. All that remains are the low inner walls and traces of two earth banks that once encircled it. Below is a later square dry-stone building known as a skeo: the wind blew through the gaps and dried meat and fish hanging inside. Inland, look for mounds of stones, made with stones removed from the fields and known as clearance cairns.

4 Walk on along the west side of the Bay of Brough. Pass through a gate and continue along the beach. Here on rocks in the bay, many seals haul out, others come very near the shore and watch. Look for sanderling, ringed plover and turnstones busy along the shoreline. Enjoy the magnificent view along Bluemull Sound, where the deep blue sea turns white as it licks against the stacks, jagged boulders and skerries.

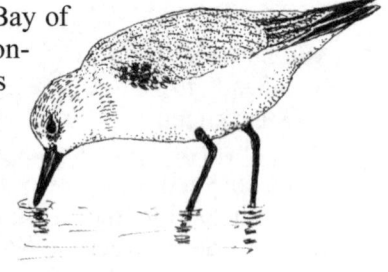

Sanderling

5 Head on across a shingle spit. Keep to the seaward side of the Loch of Papil to join a track running inland. Carry on where the track becomes metalled to pass the school. At the Y-junction, turn right and stride the narrow road between sheep pastures. Bear left with the road. Ignore the next right turn opposite the pleasingly restored Haa of Houlland, a fine house built in the mid-18th century, and take the next one to rejoin your vehicle.

Autumn Gentian

Practicals

Type of walk: *Moderate walking all the way. A pleasing short walk along sandy bays and over dramatic cliffs.*

Distance:	3 miles/5km
Time:	2 hours
Maps:	OS Explorer 470/Landranger 1

22

Gutcher, Yell

Park near the pier, where there is a café and good facilities, having followed the signs for the Gutcher ferry, grid ref 549993. To access the island, follow the directions given in walk 20.

Burra Ness iron-age broch stands 12 feet high on the seaward side. Its wall is very thick. All around the grass is a bright green, evidence that the land was under cultivation for a long time.

Sand Wick Bay is well known for otters. Approach quietly. Watch for a small head above the water. If you see an otter and it has a fish, it may lie on its back to deal with it. Then it will dive, its body and then its tail following the head with perfect co-ordination of movement. Seeing your first otter is a magical moment.

Burra Ness Broch, Yell

1 Just beyond the cafe take an unsigned path on the right to stroll south, inside the fence. Pass a crofthouse and then a house, beyond which is a mound of stones, once the site of a medieval chapel. To the left lies the island of Linga. Continue past a ruined crofthouse to climb the next fence. Walk right to see a standing stone, five feet tall, heavily encrusted with lichen. Stride over the pastures of the shallow cliffs which, in summer, resound with the songs of skylarks. Wheatears flit about the tufts of grass and great and arctic skuas sail overhead.

2 Carry on for over a mile along the low cliffs, taking care as you begin the descent to Sand Wick Bay, where you might spot an otter. Cross the Burn of Sandwick and pass another ruined crofthouse and carry on round the bay. Towards the end, go over the shingle spit that has lovely sand to the seaward side. Ahead lies the Burra Ness broch, proudly overlooking Colgrave Sound to the island of Fetlar. Here you will wish to pause.

3 Return round Sand Wick Bay and cross the burn. Look for a gate in the fence and pass through. Continue uphill in the direction of the chimney pots of North Sandwick, which you can just glimpse. Ascend the pastures, making sure to shut all gates, to come to the start of the road. Head on along the narrow road as it crosses the moorland. Soon Gutcher comes into view and you might spot one of the two ferries, from Unst and from Fetlar, approaching the pier. At the crossroads, turn right to descend the hill to return to your vehicle.

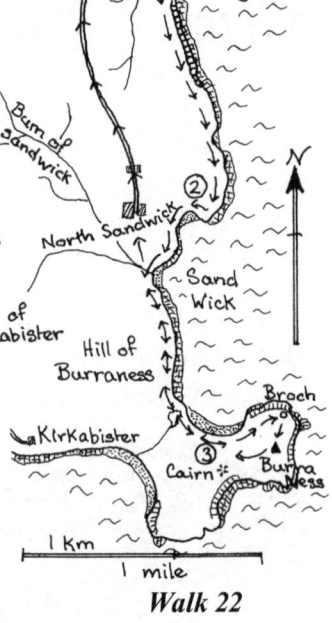

Walk 22

Otter with fish

Practicals

Type of walk: *Generally easy walking all the way.*

Distance: 5½ miles/9km
Time: 3 hours or more if otter-watching
Maps: OS Explorer 470/OS Landranger 1

23

Loch of Snarravoe, Unst

Drive along the A968 from the ferry terminal at Belmont for a mile. At the brow of the hill park in a convenient grassy area beside the road, after a right bend beyond the Loch of Snarravoe, grid ref 574017.

Unst is Shetland's most northerly island and the third largest. It is reached by a car and passenger ferry from Gutcher on the Island of Yell. The crossing takes 10 minutes and the boat runs regularly, every day.

Go through the entrance to the ruined **12th century church of St Olaf's** and walk to the end. Look under the lintel of the tiny window on your right to see a carving of a fish. Close by the lintel is a badly eroded tombstone. It marks the place where a 16th century Bremen merchant, Segebad Detken, was buried. Details of the inscription, now gone, are to be found in the Pier House museum (a restored Hanseatic bod) at Symbister on Whalsay. Look in the churchyard for a gravestone of another Bremen merchant, for several small stone crosses and for the headstone of Peter Harper, which carries a quaint legend.

Boardastubble Standing Stone, Unst

1 From the grassy parking area, walk back to the end of the crash barrier, now on your right. Take the track, running downhill, north, towards the head of the Loch of Snarravoe, close to where you have parked, and follow it around the head of the the Loch of Snarravoe and on

79

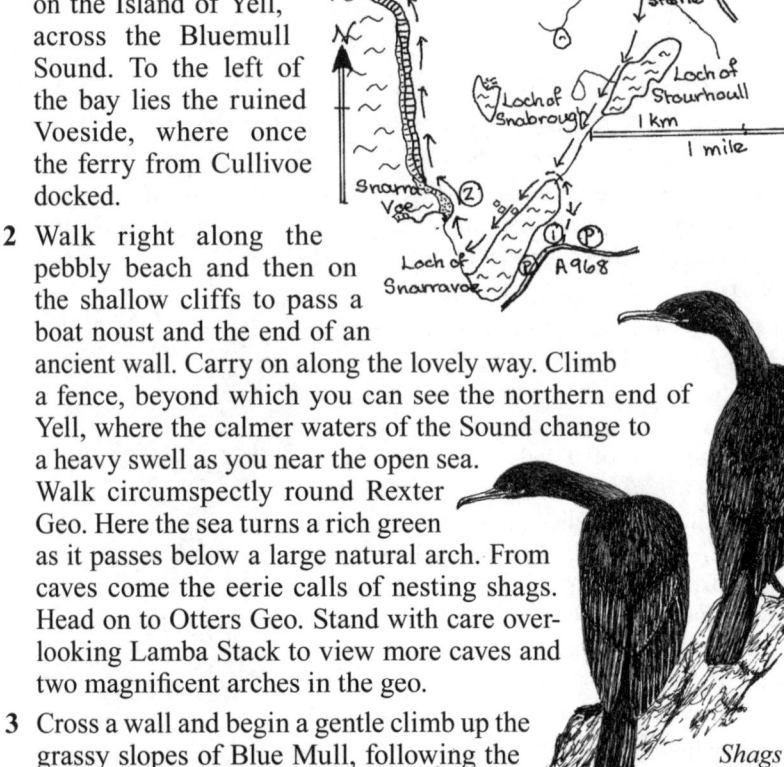

Walk 23

to bear right, crossing a wet area, to the edge of Snarra Voe. From here there is a pleasing view of Cullivoe and its white painted church of St Olaf, on the Island of Yell, across the Bluemull Sound. To the left of the bay lies the ruined Voeside, where once the ferry from Cullivoe docked.

2   Walk right along the pebbly beach and then on the shallow cliffs to pass a boat noust and the end of an ancient wall. Carry on along the lovely way. Climb a fence, beyond which you can see the northern end of Yell, where the calmer waters of the Sound change to a heavy swell as you near the open sea. Walk circumspectly round Rexter Geo. Here the sea turns a rich green as it passes below a large natural arch. From caves come the eerie calls of nesting shags. Head on to Otters Geo. Stand with care overlooking Lamba Stack to view more caves and two magnificent arches in the geo.

3   Cross a wall and begin a gentle climb up the grassy slopes of Blue Mull, following the good path to the top. Then descend gently to a wide grassy flat defended by rocks, with a dramatic view over Lunda Wick and along the north-west coast of the island. Bear right round The Nev, to come to the remains of a small, possibly iron-age, watchtower. Walk on well above the shore to pass the other end of the wall passed on your approach to Blue Mull. Cross below an extensive wall and walk the short turf to visit the ruined 12th century church of St Olaf – the gate is on the far wall of the cemetery.

Shags

4 Continue round the coast, crossing the glorious sands of Lunda Wick. Climb the pebbles at the far end and step across a small stream to go through a gate in a fence. Head straight up, with the fence to your right, to another gate through the fence. Beyond bear left to cross a wet area. Cross another fence and keep walking left until you reach Underhoull, the site of a Norse settlement. Excavations revealed a longhouse with a small area for animals at the south end. Climb straight up the hill and cross a stile into the remains of the Broch of Underhoull defended by a double rampart and two quite deep 'moats' bridged by a causeway. The Vikings removed the broch's stone to build their dwellings. From the broch continue ahead to the fence and walk right to the road.

Butterwort

5 Turn right along the quiet way. Ignore the turn to Burragarth and continue on for ½ mile to turn right along another narrow road towards a large standing stone, Boardastubble (battle-axe shape). Then cross the road and climb the track, which leads to a gate on the skyline. To your left lies the Loch of Stourhoull, where you might spot a red-throated diver. Beyond the gate, turn left to pass through another. Bear right and continue uphill and walk to the right of a ruined crofthouse. Walk on descending steadily left, past another ruin. Beyond stretches the Loch of Snarravoe. Keep to its west side to join the track taken at the start of the walk and continue uphill to rejoin your vehicle.

Practicals

Type of walk: *A walk full of evidence of Shetland's ancient past. Easy walking all the way.*

Distance:	6miles/9.8km
Time:	3–4 hours
Maps:	OS Explorer 470/OS Landranger 1

24

Muckle Flugga, Unst

Park in the area designated for the walk, grid ref 612149. To get to Unst, follow the instructions given for Walk 23. Leave the ferry by the only road, the A968, and continue. Near Haroldswick, look for the sign directing you left to Burrafirth. Beyond, almost at the end of the road, the right branch leads to the Visitor Centre, a large white elegant house, where the warden of the Hermaness Nature Reserve lives. The left branch leads up to the parking area for the walk and an information board, plus leaflets.

Thomas and David Stevenson, who started work in 1855, built **Muckle Flugga lighthouse** to protect ships during the Crimean War. It is 64ft/20m high and has 103 steps. The keepers lived in a separate shore station when off duty, the large house seen as you approach the car park. It was sold when the lighthouse became automated in March 1995. Part of it houses the Visitor Centre at the entrance to the reserve, which is managed by Scottish Natural Heritage.

Muckle Flugga from Hermaness

The lighthouse sits on a jagged outcrop, one of a **series of sea stacks** that make up some of the most northerly bits of rock in the British Isles. The only land north is Out Stack. All sit in the path of the Atlantic storms.

1. From the parking area, pass through two gates and climb the distinct well-made track through the heather. Soon waymarker posts, topped with green paint, guide you on your way. Descend steadily to cross the Burn of Winnaswarta Dale on a long footbridge and follow the track as it bears left through a sheltered hollow, then climbs a slope and divides. Go on left, following the posts beside the burn, the track now superbly boarded all across the moor. Here, at the right time of the year, you pass through the territories of golden plover, wheatear, skylark, oyster-catcher and great skua. You are asked to keep to the path to avoid erosion and not to disturb this unique area of nesting birds.

2. Where the boarding ends, walk ahead for 100yds to a signpost and turn left for Toolie. During the breeding season nothing prepares you for what awaits as you near the very high cliffs: first the noise, then the smell, and finally the sight of thousands of gannets nesting on the sheer cliffs which are brilliant white from guano. As you stroll left along the precipitous cliffs you see the rock ledges lined with more birds. The nests are made of turf or seaweed and lined with all sorts of oddments. Walk on in the same direction, watching for puffins as they glide in with red legs splayed. They land close to their burrows and then disappear into them. Further round the cliffs, where there are even more gannets, look down, with care, to see rows of

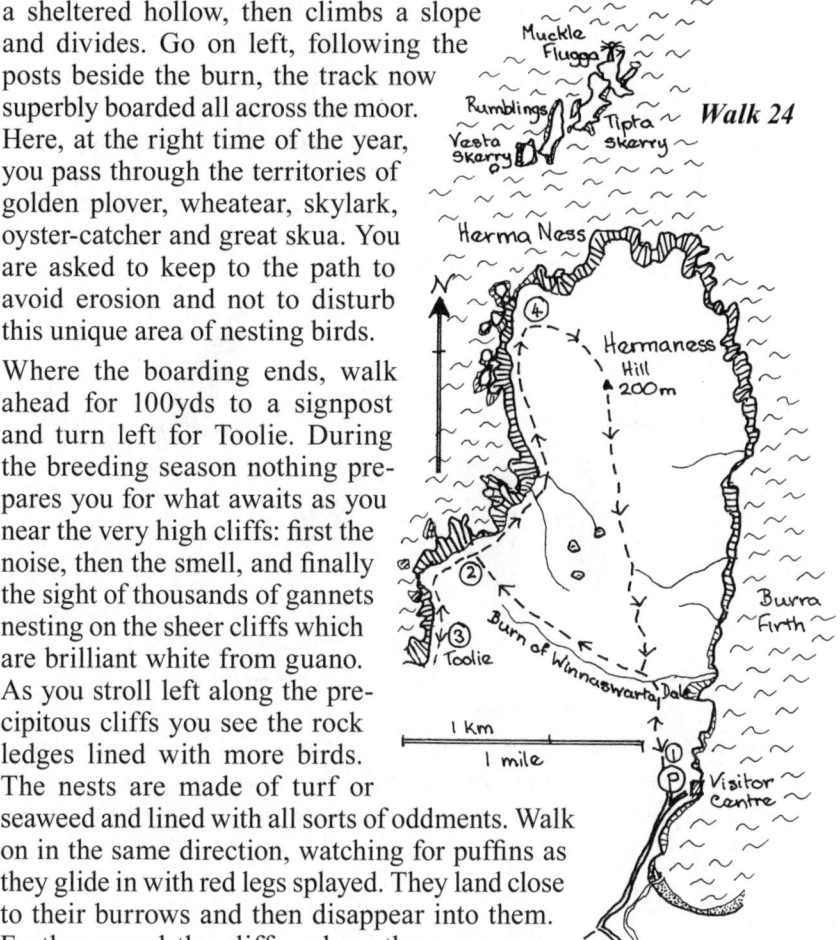

guillemots, all facing into the cliff. Fulmars nest on any grassy ledge, among the thrift. Here a few kittiwakes reside. Through all these birds, pairs of great skuas dive, looking for suitable victims.

3 Return to the signpost. Ignore your outward track and continue north along the cliffs. Drop down a steep grassy slope to cross a narrow stream. Beyond, the cliffs are pocked with puffin burrows and in season the comical-looking birds continually come and go. Soon you can glimpse the sturdy, seemingly stumpy lighthouse on Muckle Flugga, beloved by photographers, who carry their tripods over the peaty tops. Follow the waymarks as they lead you inland up the lower slopes of Hermaness Hill for a safe dramatic view of the skerries. Beyond lies Out Stack, the most northerly point of Great Britain.

4 When you can bear to leave this glorious point in your walk, return by your outward route or follow the green-topped posts up Hermaness Hill and then descend over the heather moorland. Do not stray from the path into the boggy environs. Use the duckboards over the peat hags and be grateful to the volunteers who have made the walk so pleasant. On joining the outward path by the burn, bear left and follow the waymarked route to the parking area.

Gannets

Practicals

Type of walk: *Long and challenging though the way is eased by good waymarking and well-cared-for tracks and paths. It is every ornithologist's dream – at the right time of the year, mid May to mid July.*

Distance: 6 miles/9.8km
Time: 3–4 hours
Maps: OS Explorer 470/Landranger 1

25

Horse Mill of Hagdale and Keen of Hamar, Unst

Park in the layby, on the left, at the end of the narrow road signed Littlehamar and Keen of Hamar National Nature Reserve (NNR), grid ref 641096. Access this from the Belmont terminal on Unst by the A968 to Baltasound. Continue on for just under a mile to take, on a sharp corner, the signposted right-turn.

In the disused workings, **chromite of iron**, generally referred to as **chromite**, used in explosives, metal plating and yellow paint, was quarried, on and off, from the 1850s until 1944. Horses trod the mill on a paved way at the base of the wall, turning the large stones, to grind the chromite ore. A small stream still runs into the stone socket onto to the revolving stones, where the water flushed away the lighter crushed rock, leaving the heavy chromite in the pan. The Horse Mill has been recently restored by the Shetland Amenity Trust – but one of the stones is now vertical.

Serpentine rock weathers to form a field of stones. Such an area is almost devoid of vegetation because the rock is unable to retain water and also because of its mineral content.

Horse Mill of Hagdale

But look carefully for small-scattered clumps of the rare Norwegian sandwort, a protected species. Look also for the even rarer Shetland mouse-ear chickweed, also alpine scurvy grass, moss campion, thrift, club-moss and the northern fen orchid.

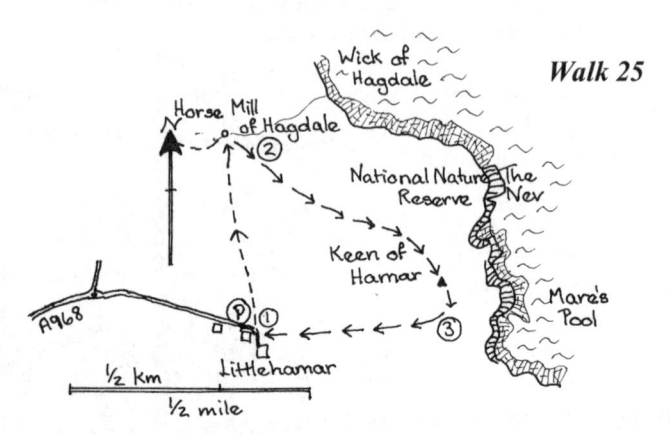

Shetland mouse-ear

Walk 25

1. From the parking area, pass through a small gate to walk along a wide cattle drove. At the next gate enter the NNR and carry on. A field gate gives access to a boggy sloping pasture, where you go straight ahead to a tall post. Go on ahead over a short stretch of rough ground to reach the partially restored circular stone horse mill, where you will want to linger.

2. Leave the mill and walk, east, across the pasture towards a stile in the fence, which gives access to the foot of the Keen of Hamar National Nature Reserve: hamar meaning a rocky outcrop on a hillside. Climb steadily over the serpentine rock to the top over this stark stone field, which looks the way much of Britain probably

looked at the end of the Ice Age. There is a fine view north to the Hill of Clibberswick and south to the island of Balta.

3 Walk right to a fence. Cross a stile and walk right, downhill, with the fence to your right and a ruined wall to your left. Where they separate continue downhill, straight ahead. At the bottom of the field, pass through the gate into the car park.

Wheatear

Arctic Sandwort

Practicals

Type of walk: *Fairly easy walking. A botanist's dream.*

Distance: 1½ miles/2.5km
Time: 1 hour
Maps: OS Explorer 470/Landranger 1

26

Muness Castle, Unst

Follow the instructions for Walk 23 to reach the Island of Unst. Leave the ferry by the A968, the only road, and take the first right turn, the B9084, signposted Muness Castle. Continue through picturesque Uyeasound, once a busy herring port, past Easter Loch via a causeway, and on through Clivocast. Look for a standing stone close to the road on the right, with Skuda Sound beyond. Ignore all right turns until you reach the castle. Park tidily on a grassy area opposite the castle, grid ref 629011. No key is needed. There are torches in a cupboard in the castle. Now also there are information boards instead of leaflets.

Muness Castle was built in 1592 by Laurence Bruce, half-brother to Robert Stewart, illegitimate son of James V, and was inhabited until 1699. It is oblong-shaped and has step gabling and round towers. It has been partially restored and is a magical place in which to wander. Each chamber has been labelled.

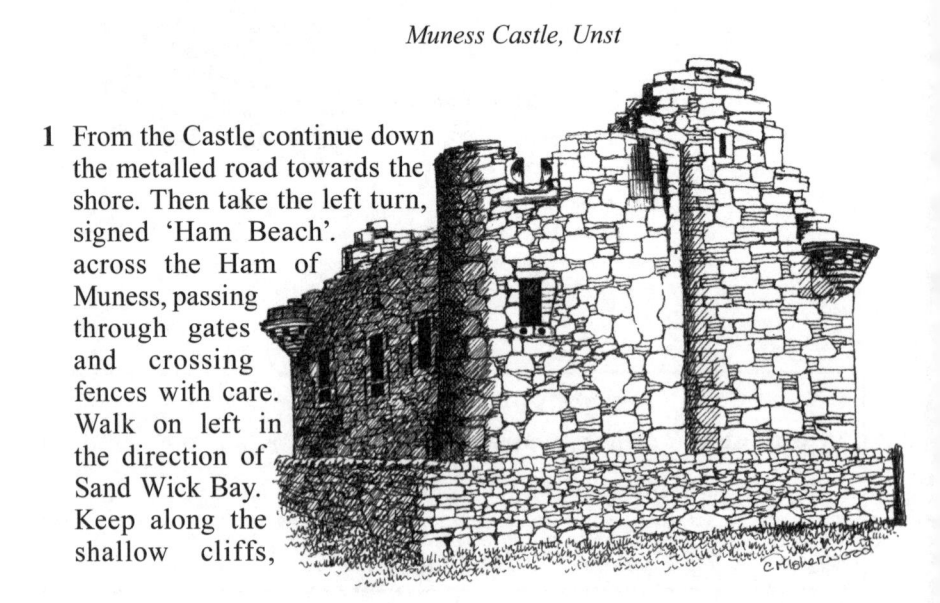

Muness Castle, Unst

1. From the Castle continue down the metalled road towards the shore. Then take the left turn, signed 'Ham Beach', across the Ham of Muness, passing through gates and crossing fences with care. Walk on left in the direction of Sand Wick Bay. Keep along the shallow cliffs,

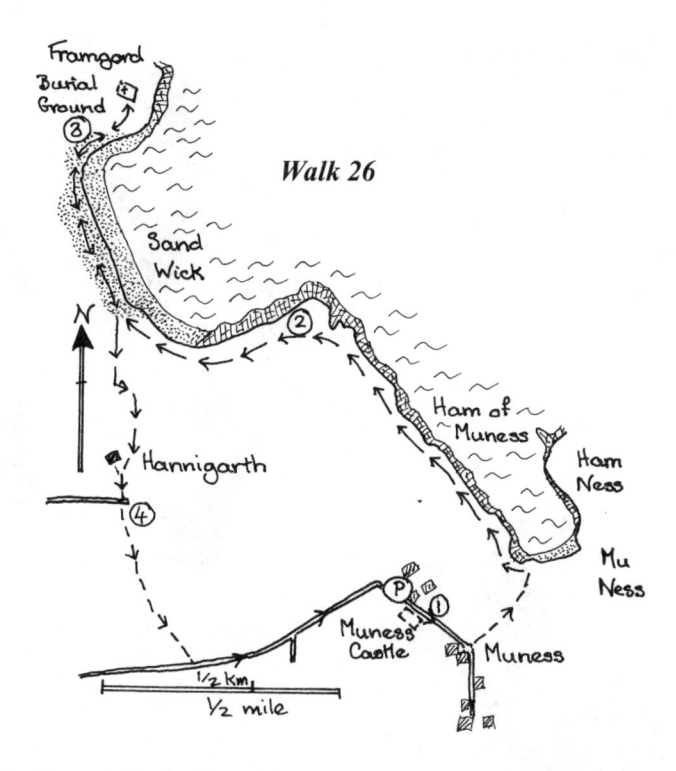

which are frequently indented by geos. Go on past a ruined medieval building, which resembles a miniature castle. Carry on to take the stile on to the lovely white-sand bay. Here great blue rollers turn to turquoise, topped with surf, as they come roaring in. You will wish to linger.

2 Cross the sands, over silver weed, to a gate at the far end of the bay. Head on above the shore towards a sturdy walled enclosure. On the far side is the entrance to the little chapel and burial ground of Framgord. Wander at will through this peaceful corner. Look for the ribbed gravestones and ancient stone crosses. Many headstones make sad reading. Here grow blue, white and pink bluebells in spring. Above the church stand ruined croft houses.

3 Return to the bay and walk the wind-rippled sand, beside the fence on your right. Here great sand mounds covered with glass-wort project eerily. At the end of the fence, turn inland to walk beside another. Continue to the corner of two fences, turn left and keep to the left of a cottage, Hannigarth, to a stile to an access track. Walk ahead to another stile to a metalled road, which you cross. Pass through the gate

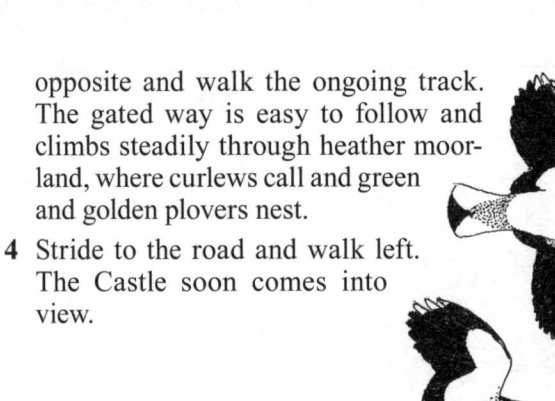

opposite and walk the ongoing track. The gated way is easy to follow and climbs steadily through heather moorland, where curlews call and green and golden plovers nest.

4 Stride to the road and walk left. The Castle soon comes into view.

Lapwings (Green Plovers)

Red Campion

Practicals

Type of walk: *Easy walking all the way.*

Distance: 4½miles/7.4km
Time: 2 hours
Maps: OS Explorer 470/Landranger 1

27

Loch of Funzie, Fetlar

Park in the car park by Loch Funzie, grid ref 656900. Access this by the free ro-ro ferry from Gutcher on Yell or Belmont on Unst to Oddsta on Fetlar. Then drive on along the B9088 almost to the end of the road. For ferry bookings contact Burravoe 01957 722259.

Fetlar lies south of the Island of Unst and measures about five miles by two and a half miles. It is a green island with very little peat. The grass provides rich grazing for many sheep. The northern part of the island is heath, which supports a wealth of plant life and birds. Fetlar once supported a population of 900. Today it is a permanent home to 50.

View towards the Snap, Fetlar.

Red-necked phalaropes are summer visitors to Loch of Funzie, nesting in small scattered colonies. They arrive in early June and seldom remain after the end of August. The breeding plumage is a combination of slate-grey, fox-red and white. Nests are well concealed and after the four eggs are laid, the males do all of the incubation and the rearing of the chicks.

Red-necked Phalarope

Walk 27

1. From the parking area follow the blue waymarks to pass Loch of Funzie (pronounced Finnie). Here, red-throated divers and red-necked phalaropes breed and you are asked not to walk round the loch to avoid disturbing them. Continue to the bird hide, opened in 1989 and look out over the mire of Funzie.

2. Return to the loch and take the wide grassy track that climbs through heather to the disused coastguard look-out station. Cross right to the fence and then walk left, down the slope, over grass and heather, to the edge of the Geo of Litlaland. From here you can glimpse the sands of Tresta and gaze across to the steep cliffs of Lamb Hoga. Carry on left along the cliffs where the deformed conglomerate rock is dramatically exposed. Take great care as you reach Staves Geo, a very narrow but extremely sheer ravine where roseroot grows in profusion.

3. Move inland a short distance to see a small lochan, Croo Water, around which graze ponies with their foals. With care, return to the cliff edge of The Snap. As you walk on, look for a magnificent natural arch that has great veins of minerals slanting through the parent rock. Both

fulmars and kittiwakes nest on the ledges. Continue round Butsa. Then take a narrow path leading over the turf to a fence. Follow this down to reach the bird hide once more. Beyond, walk the waymarked path to return to the car park.

Shetland Wren

Practicals

Type of walk: *A delightful walk. Leave yourself time to enjoy the bird hide.*

Distance: 3½ miles/5.5km
Time: 2 hours or more, depending on time spent in bird hide.
Maps: OS Explorer 470/Landranger 1

28

Strandburgh Ness, Fetlar

Park at the car park at Funzie Loch, grid ref 656900. To access this, see walk 27.

Sir Arthur Nicolson built the roundhouse as a **summerhouse** and to be alone. The lower rooms were built of stone. There were four pillars at the entrance. The upper storey was built of wood. One day Sir Arthur set off on horseback from his home, Brough Lodge, near the ferry, to spend his first night in the summerhouse. As soon as he tried to sleep, he was disturbed by a loud knocking, which continued until he could stand it no longer. He returned to his stately home. When Sir Arthur spoke to the minister of the kirk about the noise, the minister suggested that it might be the spirits of the people he had evicted that were knocking. Sir Arthur never used the summerhouse again. Later the house became an office for his factor.

After walking on Fetlar you may wish to complete your trip by visiting the **Fetlar Interpretive Centre** at Houbie. Here, there is a small museum, which contains much history of the Nicolson family. Sir Arthur was the laird of Fetlar in the 1800s. He evicted many tenants to make way for sheep. The centre has many interesting letters and records to read and audio-visual presentations to view.

The Roundhouse, Fetlar

Walk 28

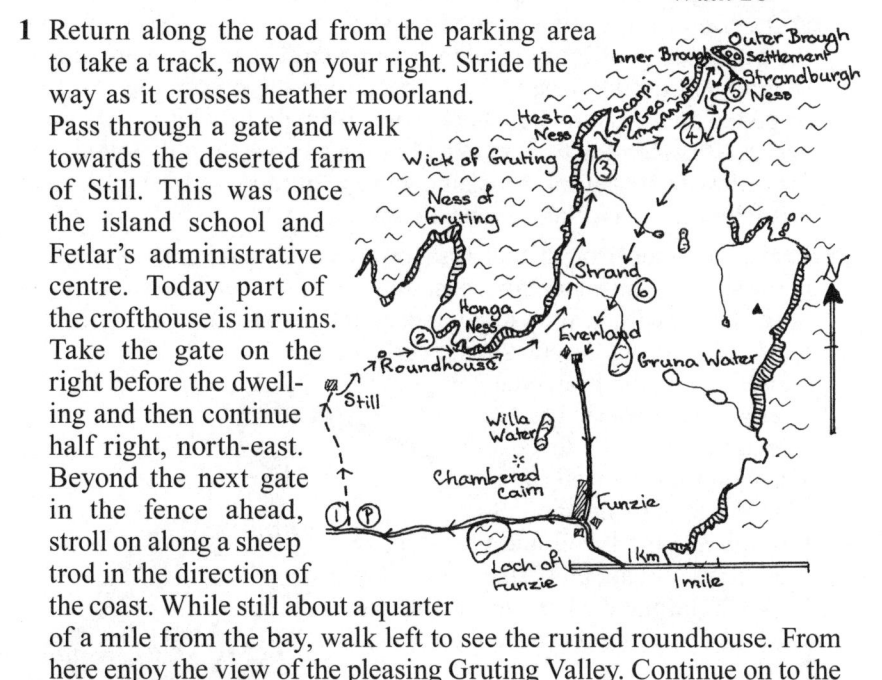

1. Return along the road from the parking area to take a track, now on your right. Stride the way as it crosses heather moorland. Pass through a gate and walk towards the deserted farm of Still. This was once the island school and Fetlar's administrative centre. Today part of the crofthouse is in ruins. Take the gate on the right before the dwelling and then continue half right, north-east. Beyond the next gate in the fence ahead, stroll on along a sheep trod in the direction of the coast. While still about a quarter of a mile from the bay, walk left to see the ruined roundhouse. From here enjoy the view of the pleasing Gruting Valley. Continue on to the beach and walk right.

2. Carry on, with care, outside the fence, along the steadily climbing cliffs. Look down on another glorious sandy bay, cross several tiny streams and walk round the end of sturdy walls built of several horizontal layers of stone topped with rows laid in the vertical. Pass the roofless Smithfield House. Go on round the end of two more walls, then look for a ruined watermill on a small stream where you might spot snipe. Go on by a plantiecrub. Be alert as you walk for the many narrow geos that slash the way.

3. Walk round the rock-strewn headland of Hesta Ness, from where you have a superb view of Unst, of the Fetlar's huge stack known as the Clett of Birrier, and of Strandburgh Ness. Stroll on around Skarpi Geo, where you might see the remains of winding gear used in the quarrying of soapstone a century ago. Now the way continues past more narrow precipitous geos that expose faces of conglomerate rock. Look for natural arches and stacks on which stand many shags.

4. Dawdle over the lovely short turf and as you climb gently the south-facing slope of Strandburgh, at the right time of the year, look for the

delicate squill turning the slope to blue. Continue to a small building at the top of the slope and then pass through the ruined walls onto the promontory of Inner Brough, where you feel as if you are almost surrounded by the ocean. Walk ahead over the grassy top, pausing in good time to view the isle of Outer Brough, to which there is no access. Between the two broughs lies the narrow Brough Sound, vey far below. To the left of the island, you can glimpse a stone wall. Here it is believed was a Norse monastic settlement.

5 Leave the Inner Brough and cross towards a fence that marches uphill to the skyline, the intervening pasture sometimes wet. Keep to the right of the fence, with heather moorland stretching away on both sides, the haunt of great and arctic skuas, curlew and whimbrel. At the brow you can glimpse Everland farmhouse; head in that direction. Cross the fence and stride on keeping well right of a large area of reedy pools. Step through a ruined wall and then over two more fences. Walk on beside a wall at the back of Smithfield where you should pick your way carefully because it can be wet here.

6 Take the left of two gates beyond the house and strike over the pasture to Everland farmhouse to join a track and then a metalled road. Carry on to the settlement of Funzie and then join the B9088 as it swings right. Stride on to the car park by the loch.

Whimbrel

Practicals

Type of walk: *Pleasing, challenging walk. Generally easy walking. Watch out for the wet, and sometimes very wet, areas. Take care on the steep cliffs.*

Distance:	6 miles/9.8km
Time:	3–4 hours
Maps:	OS Explorer 470/Landranger 1

29

Ollaberry

Park in the car park beside the Church of Scotland, Ollaberry, grid ref 369806. To access this leave Lerwick by the A970. Continue through Central Mainland to Voe and then on to Brae. Soon the road crosses Mavis Grind, a thin strip of land with the North Sea on the right and the Atlantic on the left. After 6 ½ miles/10.5km, turn right for Ollaberry. Once in the hamlet, turn right immediately, passing in front of the post office and wind left to park.

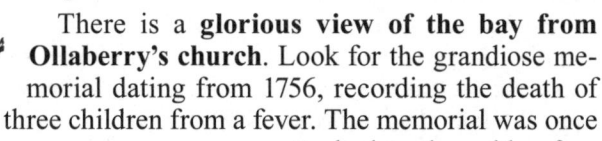

There is a **glorious view of the bay from Ollaberry's church**. Look for the grandiose memorial dating from 1756, recording the death of three children from a fever. The memorial was once attached to the gable of an earlier church. The small village has a fine 19th century pier and crane. Here, among boulders on the shore, you might see an otter.

From the Back of Ollaberry you can see **Sullom Voe Terminal**, which receives crude oil from the Brent and Ninian fields. It is pumped here through long pipelines to be processed at the terminal and then sent worldwide in huge tankers. The whole complex is pleasingly unobtrusive.

The Pier, Ollaberry

97

Walk 29

1. Visit the church. Then leave the churchyard by the gate and pass through the gate (right) signed 'Access Route'. Walk on over the pasture, with the wall of the church on your right, and go on along the low cliffs. Carry on towards Otter Hadd. Look out to see the island of Lamba, with a pristine white lighthouse on it. The way becomes steeper; heather and bilberry grow here. Head on up to the top of the hill, known as Back of Ollaberry, from where you have a good view of the Island of Yell over the Sound.

2. Drop down the slope and stroll round the promontory known as the Taing of Norwick, where the cliffs are sheer. Look for roseroot thriving in a steep ravine and butterwort in the wet flushes. Step across a burn and pass through a gate to continue above the lovely sandy bay of Nor Wick, where eiders and common gulls bathe and preen. Head on along the lower slopes of the Hill of Norwick. As you turn left along the edge of Quey Firth, you feel the sea breezes lessen as you benefit from the shelter of the Ness of the same name.

   Common Gull

3. Go ahead towards the sandy ayre. It looks inviting until you realise you are separated from it by a fast-flowing burn. This issues from the Loch of Queyfirth and flows up against the shallow cliffs on which you are walking. You might see numerous terns screaming as they fly overhead and many diving headlong after fish in the firth.

4 From here begin the steady ascent, striking diagonally left up the Hill of Ollaberry (350ft/118m). The climb goes up relentlessly but pause frequently to enjoy the great views northwards and listen for golden plovers. Stand by the trig point for more superb views. Then strike west (right) to drop down, crossing several fences to join the road from Leon. Turn left and descend through pastures bright yellow with primroses and marsh marigolds in late spring. At the T-junction turn left to walk into Ollaberry to rejoin your vehicle.

Primrose

Practicals

Type of walk: *Easy walking for most of the way. A pleasant afternoon's stroll with a steepish climb towards the end.*

Distance: 3 miles/5km
Time: 2 hours
Maps: OS Explorer 469/Landranger 3

30

Lunna

Park on the grass verge, on the left, close to the track that leads to a large well-constructed stone limekiln, shaped like a beehive, seen well in advance, grid ref 484692. To access this, leave the A970 by the B9071, signposted 'Laxo – Whalsay Ferry terminal'. The road passes near to both piers. Continue ahead alongside Vidlin Voe to Lunna.

After you have visited the limekiln (beware of nesting fulmars) return to cross the road and walk on between a tall folly, high on the hill on the right, and the magnificent 17th century Lunna House to the left. The grand house is now quiet, but in the Second World War it played a vital part in the **'Shetland Bus'** operations. It was, until 1942, the headquarters of the Norwegian resistance movement.

Lunna Kirk, built in 1753, was constructed of massive volcanic whinstone blocks from nearby. It has sandstone details round the doors and windows and two leper 'squint' holes where the afflicted could listen to the service. Look for two ancient inscribed memorial slabs, now indecipherable, incorporated into the wall of the porch. Another recalls Robert T. Hunter of Lunna who died in the early 1600s. The little church has a charming gallery.

Stanes of Stofast

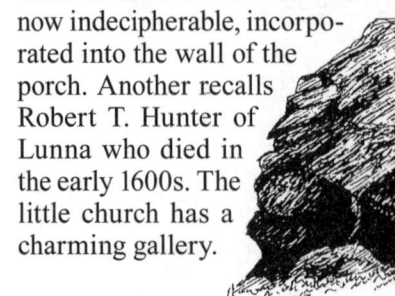

1   Continue past a ruined church-like crofthouse. This was once a private chapel for the great house. Pass through a gate in the wall and bear left to visit the charming Lunna Kirk. Walk to the shore of East Lunna and bear left to pass a bod, once the old smithy, and a man-made beach,

a wide flat area of stones where fishermen landed their fish. Close by near the shore you might see otters and common seals. Continue along the cliffs. Pause to look across to see the village of Brough on Whalsay and then the islands of Out Skerries. Cross the wall by the stone-stepped stile, with a lovely view down into Kels Wick.

2 Take care as you round the promontory known as the Taing of Kelswick, and Ramna Geo. Go by Mill Loch, which lies away to your left and is set in a grassy hollow surrounded by rocky outcrops. Cross the bay of Grut Wick, where there is no trace of the Ninian oil pipeline that comes ashore here. It runs close to Lunna House and then on to Sullom Voe terminal. Continue on and climb the stile over the fence. Keep to the left side of a lochan and stroll on. Go over a small hill to look down on the attractive South Loch of Stofast. Immediately above the loch stand the dramatic Stanes of Stofast, huge erratic boulders, believed to have been deposited by an Ice Age glacier. Head up the slope to stand by them – you will feel like a dwarf.

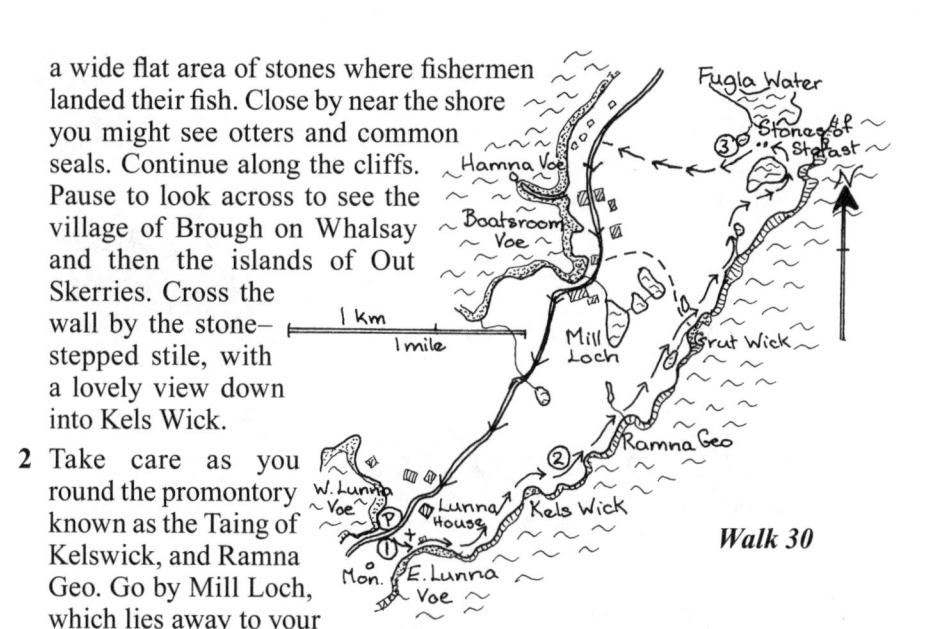

3 From here carry on along the ridge in a westerly direction. Cross the valley and head uphill to a stile, clearly visible. Cross the stile and follow the waymarked posts across the shallow valley, round a hill and down to another stile. Cross and keep ahead. Another waymark directs to a stile and the road. Turn left and begin the two-mile walk back to Lunna. Pass several ruined crofts and then the strange pebble ayre that crosses half of Hamna Voe. Stride close to a small fenced area of trees, planted in aid of Children in Need. In August enjoy the devil's bit scabious, which lines the road. Twites and starlings perch on the fences and

Walk 30

Devil's-bit Scabious

101

rock doves feed in the fields. Carry on beside Boatsroom Voe and pass a watermill on your left. Next comes the long climb uphill. At the brow you can see Lunna farm, with more trees, and then Lunna house. Continue past both and stroll on to rejoin your vehicle by the limekiln.

Rock Dove

Limekiln, Lunna

Practicals

Type of walk: *Easy walking all the way. An exhilarating six-miler with good views.*

Distance: 6 miles/9.8km
Time: 3 hours
Maps: OS Explorer 468/Landranger 2

31

Out Skerries

To reach these pleasing islands, use the ferry that leaves Vidlin in the morning, giving walkers 5–6 hours until the return afternoon sailing. Booking is essential, phone 01806 515 226. Walkers may well choose to fly in and out using the 20 minute inter-island air service from Tingwall (01595 840246). Vidlin on Vidlin Voe is reached first by the A970 and then by the well signposted B9071.

No visit to Shetland would be complete without a trip to the small group of islands known as the **Out Skerries.** They are composed of three islands: Bruray and Housay, which are connected by a bridge, and uninhabited Grunay, separated from them by a narrow strip of water. Lighthouse keepers who serviced the tall Out Skerries lighthouse, built in 1857 by the family firm of Stevenson, lived on Grunay. Today the light is automatic and the houses empty. The island is privately owned.

On the one and half hour ferry trip, look for gannets, puffins, arctic terns, black and common guillemots and porpoises. The ferry at first keeps close to Lunna Ness and then crosses to take the advantage of the shelter of Whalsay. The last stretch into the superb natural harbour of Out Skerries is very exciting.

Out Skerries Lighthouse

1. From the ferry, walk along the road and look left across the harbour to see, on a green pasture, a large stone circle, possible Bronze Age, and known as Battle Pund. It is thought that blood feuds may have been settled here in single combat. Stroll on until just before you reach a pond below a small reservoir. Here take a stile over the fence to your right. Bear right to walk above the airstrip and the aqueduct. Ahead you have a dramatic view of the lighthouse. Continue on the lovely turf towards the cliff edge. In spring the way is covered with wild flowers. Take care as you climb steadily because the cliffs are sheer. Look over to Lamba Stack, with its innumerable fulmars. Go on around the headland, from where a magnificent view opens up across to Fetlar and Yell, with Saxa Vord on Unst showing clearly.

2. Take care round Bruray Taing, where a grand rock garden stretches down to sea level and where the waters of the North Sea crash white-topped on jagged rocks. Continue along the east side of North Mouth to come to a stile in the fence on the opposite side of the small reservoir seen at the start of the walk. Strike right across the fine turf to cross Skerries Bridge, built in 1957, to Housay. Now you are in the centre of the small village where most people live. Bear right before the coast-guard hut. Walk on a few yards round the head of North Mouth, and then wind right to continue your round-island walk. Cross the fence and stroll on. Dawdle along the west side of the huge inlet, where in bad weather the ferry berths. Cross a pebble beach with a high shore of cobbles that stretches inland. Pass Vogans Voe, with Wether Holm across a narrow channel.

3. Go through a wall and continue up the slope and on. Soon you look into West Voe. As you round the small peninsula, keep well up the steepish slopes close to the cairn on North Hill. Here you are in the territory of the arctic tern. Walk on across the low-growing heather; there is no peat

Walk 31

on the Skerries and in the past islanders fetched it from neighbouring Whalsay. Wind round the head of West Voe and continue south to climb the stile in the fence (the other end of the fence crossed earlier) and walk across old cultivation strips.

4 Carry on to reach a track, which you cross. Walk behind a farm building, go over a fence and continue ahead along the low cliffs. Pass through a wall and keep round Queyin Ness, a great mass of rocky outcrops and boulders. Here, at the foot of the cliffs, the waves pound the rocks, contrasting sharply with the calm water of the Voe. Stroll on through a large area of clearance cairns and walk towards the wall on your left and go through a gap near its end. Now the promontory is very narrow and as you walk along the rocky spine, great plates and jagged ridges of rock stretch away on both sides to drop to sea level. After viewing Troli Geo with care, and the 'island' beyond, return along the finger of land and then move to the cliffs on the right where the land broadens.

5 Join a track faintly marked at first with tractor tyres and follow it until you reach the back of the school. Strike left behind the houses and join the road to visit Skerries Church – a beautifully-kept haven of peace. Continue along the road and just before the bridge turn right in the direction of the post office. Go behind the houses on the right to visit the great circle of stones, Battle Pund. Walk back to cross the bridge, pass the community hall and on to catch the ferry.

Guillemots swimming

Practicals

Type of walk: *Easy walking all the way. A delightful round-island walk.*

Distance: 7–8 miles/ 12–13km
Time: 4 hours
Maps: OS Explorer 468/Landranger 2

32

Isbister, Whalsay

Park in a large layby, almost at the end of the road, that passes the north-east corner of Loch Isbister, grid ref 581641. To access Whalsay leave the A970 just before Voe, where the ferry terminal at Laxo is well signposted. Ferries run regularly throughout the day and the attractive journey takes 30 minutes. It is always wise to book (telephone 01806 566259).

The **green island of Whalsay** lies to the east of the Mainland of Shetland. Large and small fishing boats throng the little harbour of Symbister and around it stand many colourful houses. At the far end of the island a golf course shares its quiet remoteness with sheep, the airstrip and many nesting waders. The island probably derives its name from an old Norse word meaning Whale island.

Yoxie Neolithic Homestead, Whalsay

1 Walk back along the road, where the smell of burning peat hangs in the air. Where the road swings left to the side of the loch, stride ahead along a track, which is reinforced with gneiss. Just before the end of the track, pass through a gate on the left and stroll on along a grassy track. Several plantiecrubs line the way. Over to your right you can see the sheer cliffs of Noss.

Plantiecrub

2 Take the right fork when the track branches and continue climbing gently. Almost at the top of the hill, Gamla Vord, bear right and, just beyond a round stone structure, look for the remains of a Neolithic chambered cairn. It has a small rectangular hollow, lined with boulders of gneiss. Pause to enjoy the views of the harbour and across to Ronas Hill on Mainland. Look ahead to where the walk continues, the finger of land, north-east Whalsay, stretching out into the sea.

3 As you continue along the centre ridge look first for the Loch Vatshoull and then West Loch of Skaw, both to your left. Stride on over the grassy top, keep to the left of the airstrip and then to the left of the small East Loch of Skaw. As you go you might hear the trill of dunlin as they fly overhead. Ahead lie the greens of the well-tended Whalsay golf course. Go on along the pleasing low cliffs on the west side of the promontory until you come opposite to the Inner Holm of Skaw and can see the remains of an old chapel. Wind right, south-east, along the wild shore and on round Skaw Taing.

4 Carry on along the east coast of the island, which is riven with deep geos. Look out to sea, left, to see gannets dive. Continue beside the fence and then below the airstrip. Once past the golf course, head on along the close-cropped turf. Go

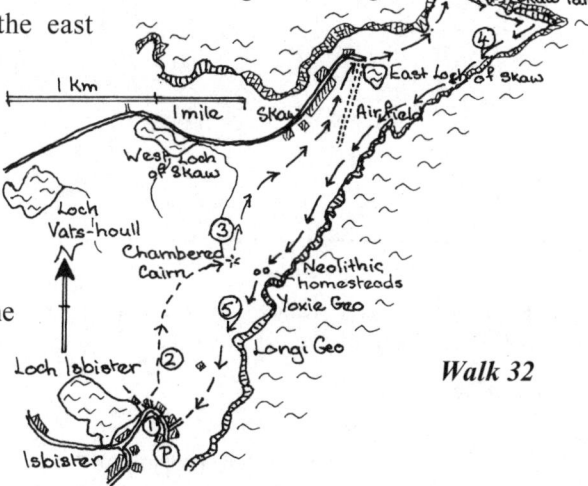

Walk 32

on over Pettigarth's field, a slightly raised area, with boulders, on the slope of Yoxie Geo. Here are the remains of two buildings, thought to be Neolithic homesteads, In one you can trace the outlines of an entrance to two compartments. On the ridge above is the chambered cairn visited on your outward route. Here this flourishing small community would have buried their dead.

5 Go on beside a fence. Pass Longi Geo. Stride on and soon the Loch of Isbister comes into view. To the left are bright green fenced fields in great contrast to the rough grass of the headland. Look for the grassy track leading to where you have parked. Drop down the slope. Keep to the right of a wall to join the reinforced track that brings you to your vehicle.

Dunlin

Practicals

Type of walk: *Easy walking all the way. A grand walk for sea views and for seeking out ancient sites.*

Distance:	5 miles/8km
Time:	3 hours
Maps:	OS Explorer 468/Landranger 2

33

Ward o' Clett, Whalsay

To reach Whalsay, follow the instructions at the beginning of Walk 32. Leave your vehicle near the pier, grid ref 536625.

The population of the island is about 1,000 and the main settlement is Symbister. Its harbour shelters the island's renowned modern fishing fleet, owned by the island fishermen. The Norse people called it 'whale' island because of its hump back – the Ward o' Clett.

1 Walk west to pass a modern fish processing factory. Continue over the fence and head on along a track towards a quarry. Climb the slope to the right of it and press on to the side of the squat white lighthouse. Head on up left, inland, to a telegraph pole on the hilltop, beside which are the remains of a chambered cairn.

Hanseatic Bod, Symbister, Whalsay

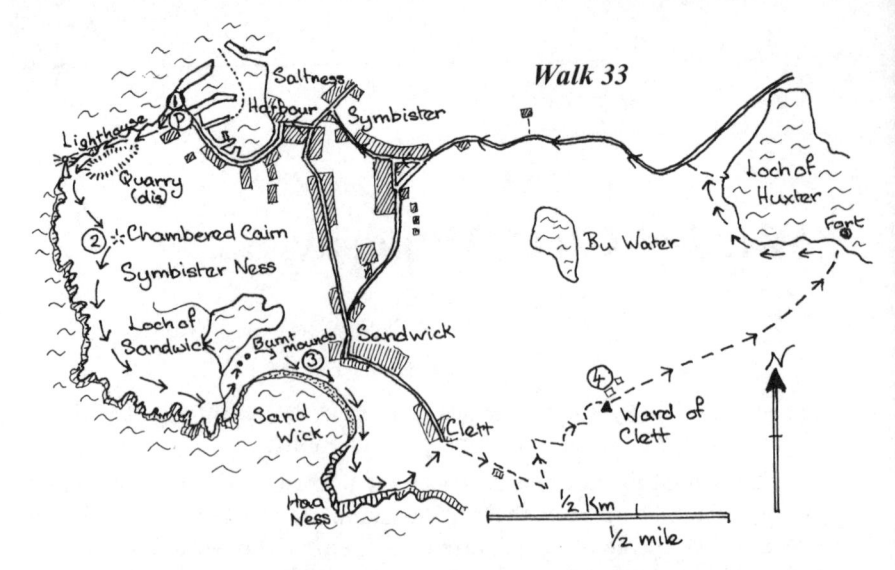

2 Return to the cliff edge and walk on along the pleasing way. Take care as you round the many geos. Continue to the edge of the lovely bay of Sand Wick. Move inland to the side of Sandwick Loch, passing a burnt mound. There is also a kidney-shaped burnt mound beside the loch. From the loch you can see the fine Symbister House towering over the small town. It was built by Robert Bruce, the laird of Whalsay in 1830. It belonged to the Bruce family until the 1920s. Today it is the local high school.

3 Return to the shore and then go on along the low sea cliffs. Stroll the next pebbly beach, where you might spot turnstones. Press on along the low cliffs, cross the next fence and keep on over Haa Ness. When you reach a wall about fifty yards before a burn, cross the fence on the left and walk over pasture towards the houses at Clett. Pass through a farm gate and on to a wicket gate to the road, where you turn right. Where the road ceases to be metalled, head on. Ignore the track going off right. At a large farm building, follow the reinforced track as it swings left and begins to climb, zig-zagging upwards towards the triangulation point

Starlings

on your right, on the Ward o' Clett (393ft/119m). From here there is a glorious view of the east coast of Shetland.

4 Walk on to a gated fence, passing several large disused buildings. Look down to see the Iron-Age fort on the Loch of Huxter. Descend the faint green path down over the slopes to come to the side of the large loch. A stone causeway connects the shore with the fort. Ferns thrive in its shelter and starlings nest between the stones. Turn left to walk the often wet way along the shore to join the road and turn left to Symbister. Look out for Pier House, a restored Hanseatic bod, now used as a museum. Walk on towards the ferry to rejoin your vehicle.

Fort, Loch of Huxter

Practicals

Type of walk: *Exhilarating. A walk through an interesting corner of Whalsay*

Distance: 4½ miles/7.2km
Time: 2 hours
Maps: OS Explorer 468/Landranger 2

34

Setter, Weisdale

Park in large space to the right before Setter House, grid ref 397546. To access this leave the A970 by the B9075, heading west. At Setter the B-road makes a sharp left turn but continue right to the parking space.

Weisdale Mill was built in 1855. Water from the dam, across the road, drove the mill, which served a large area. The grain for milling was brought in boats to the head of the Voe and then transported inland. The ground floor has an area for refreshments. Alas, all the old machinery has long gone and therefore the mill cannot be restored to its past glory.

At one time Shetland seemed **bereft of trees** although pollen analysis of the peat shows that once it was covered with pine and birch trees. The woodland at Weisdale seemed to provide the only trees in this rather barren land. It was of great delight to bird watchers and twitchers. Today there are small areas of trees shielding modern dwellings

Ruined Crofts, Weisdale

from the prevailing winds. Many of the trees are conifers and they show wind-burn but they are still thriving and are a pleasure to see. Gardens in Lerwick and other settlements have sturdy bushes and low-growing trees and these soften the rather dour grey buildings. There are also new plantations of native trees such as birch, willow and alder. Encouraged by the Shetland Amenities Trust these have been planted in sheltered areas and seem to be growing well.

1. Go back 20m to take a track now on your right. Then bear right to pass a ruined crofthouse and continue towards a small plantation of firs and pines. Walk uphill by the fence with the trees to your right. From the conifers comes a strange sound for the island, the cacophony of a rookery. On the edge of the pines grow several willows and hawthorn bushes. At the end of the plantation cross the fence, turn left and stroll on along the same contour. Ahead you can see Fitful Head and the southern end of Mainland. Cross another fence and walk above a second plantation, where grow pine and larch. Stride on to a third, planted with a band of rowan, alder, birch and willow edging the mature conifers.

2. Walk on above the fence to go through a gate above a ruined crofthouse. Follow a narrow path down to the next ruin where it becomes an old track way, which must have linked all the houses and probably led down to the church. Head for the gabled church at the head of Weisdale Voe by dropping diagonally left. Go through another gate. Before a rocky hill, climb a wooden piece of fence into a field. Walk down towards the church with the fence on your left. Go through a gate onto a track above the river. Turn right, through two more gates. Cross the old bridge to join the B9075 and turn left to visit the 19th century church.

3. Go on along the quiet road to Weisdale Mill and perhaps visit. Then stroll on and just before the farm, at the start of the last pasture on the right, look for a burnt mound, large enough for cooking food and

perhaps for saunas. Beyond the farm, in more woodland, is another rookery, this time set high in sycamores. Then you pass the many trees about Kergord House, planted in the 19th century. Look for elm, copper beech, sycamore, rowan, ash, willow, white-beam and horsechestnut. Stroll on past the 19th century laird's house. Once it was known as Flemington and the mill just passed was part of the estate. The house was built of stone from the crofthouses emptied during The Clearances. In 1940 it became the administrative centre for the activities of the 'Shetland Bus'. In 1945 the house was renamed Kergord.

4 Continue along the road to rejoin your vehicle.

Rook

Practicals

Type of walk: *Easy waking all the way although it can be wet in places. An inland expedition providing a great contrast to the many cliff walks of Shetland.*

Distance:	3½ miles/5km
Time:	2 hours
Maps:	OS Explorer 467/Landranger 3

35

Aith Ness, Bressay

Park in a reinforced area, at the end of the good track, close to the last house on the right, Bruntland, grid ref 511427. Access Bressay by the frequent ferry that leaves Albert Building in the centre of Lerwick. Drive ahead from the terminal following the signpost for Noss. At Uphouse, ignore the right turn for the smaller island (Noss) and continue ahead in the direction for Setter. When the farmhouse comes into view, drive along an un-signposted reinforced track, going off left through the heather moorland. Ignore the right turn for Swart Houll and go on down towards the Loch of Aith.

The **Island of Bressay** lies three-quarters of a mile east of Lerwick, across the Bressay Sound. The shelter it provides has given Lerwick a fine natural harbour. The island's population of about 350 live on the west coast, looking across to the capital. It was not always so. Three times as many people lived on the island early in the 19th century, mainly on the east coast, but they were cleared in the 1870s to make room for sheep.

The island is composed mainly of **Old Red Sandstone** and from this rock the many walls are constructed. They enclose the narrow roads, and in summer the verges are bright with colourful flowers. The sandstone has eroded into gently rounded hills and dramatic sea cliffs and caves.

Aith, Bressay

115

1 Walk on along the track to pass through a gate. Beyond, head over left to follow a good sheep trod over the shallow cliffs of Aith Voe, where, earlier in the century, herring was processed into fishmeal. Carry on over the short turf. Go round a small bay to pass a ruined house and the remains of fortifications used in the first World War. Just offshore lies the Holm of Gunnista. Continue round Elvis Voe, where the thin-layered sandstone forms a flat path and stroll on over a carpet of thrift. Just before you reach the islands of Inner Score and Outer Score, look in the cliffs for the fascinating conglomerate rock with granite and quartzite embedded in the sandstone.

2 Continue on along the east coast of Ness. Cross a delightful ayre with turquoise water over the sand on the seaward side and a deep blue loch on the other. On both sides of the ayre you might spot eider ducks. Then begin the climb up the cliffs of Score Hill. Stroll on with care to walk round Blue Geo, where sandstone was quarried to pave the streets of Lerwick and for building and roofing. Lerwick Town Hall is built with Bressay stone.

3 Stride on around the Minni of Aith. Drop down the slope to pass through and beside the well-built walls of a ruined crofthouse (Aith) and go on until you rejoin the track taken at the outset of the walk. Stroll on with the Loch of Aith to your right to rejoin your vehicle.

Walk 35

Eiders

Practicals

Type of walk: *Easy walking all the way. Care is required on the cliffs. A pleasing walk with dramatic cliffs and good views.*

Distance:	4 miles/6.5km
Time:	2 hours
Maps:	OS Explorer 466/Landranger 4

36

Kirkabister Lighthouse, Bressay

Park in a largish space, on the left, before the gates to the lighthouse, grid ref 489378, taking care not to block the turning space. To reach Bressay follow the instructions at the start of Walk 35. Drive off the ferry and take the first right turn. Just beyond a sharp turn in the road take the next right turn, signposted Kirkabister, and continue to the end of the road.

    The **lighthouse**, built on this southern tip of the island, was constructed by the Stevenson family and is now fully automated. It is a welcoming sight when approaching on the Lerwick ferry through the Bressay Sound.

    After leaving the pier, look left to see the fine **Gardie house**, with its walled garden. It was built in 1724 from local sandstone and is the home of the laird's son.

Kirkabister Lighthouse, Bressay

Walk 36

1 Pass through the gate to the left of the lighthouse and begin the steady climb over the flower-covered turf. Look left to see a ruined settlement, with old walls and turf dykes, on the slopes above. Look back down for a good view of the lighthouse standing on its splendid natural arch. Ahead you can see Sumburgh Head. Continue upwards, with the fence to the right. Look over the glorious busy Sound to Lerwick, an attractive grey and red stone town with houses climbing up hills and ending neatly at the edge of the frowning moorland.

2 After the long pull up Ord Cliff (400ft/122m), pause again to enjoy the pleasing view. Here the impressive cliffs are much eroded. Continue over the heather and then descend steadily keeping beside the cliffside fence until you reach a wall. Walk inland to go through a gate and descend over grass to pass a ruined homestead and a sheep pen to cross the Burn of Veng, which drops seawards in small falls. Cross the burn that flows out of Sand Vatn, which continues to the cliff edge and plummets in white tresses to the sea.

3 Stroll on over The Bard, which juts finger-like out into the sea. At Bard Head, stands the remains of a huge rusting gun from the first World War. Close by the cliff edge is all that remains of the gantry that eventually was successful at hauling the gun up from a barge far below. Walk on along the grassy headland to view Stoura Clett, with its fine

arch, then carry on to the small Loch of Seligeo, with the dramatic Seli Geo away to the right. Then begin to descend to continue round a bay where sandstone flags lie in a huge jumble, remnants of earlier quarrying. Here you might see ringed plover scurrying over the turf.

4 Go round the next geo, which is really just a lovely rock garden, and then climb the steep slopes ahead. Press on in the direction of a ruined crofthouse, before the Loch of Grimsetter, to walk inland on the same contour line to cross a wall. Go on past several ruined crofthouses, a sad reminder of the days of the Clearances. At the back of the one nearest to the loch look for the souterrain, an earth house. Head on diagonally left to a gate in the wall. Beyond, lies a good track well reinforced. Stride on, right, to the side of the Loch of Brough. Half way along the side of the loch, turn left and climb the slope beside a drainage ditch, walking a grassy swathe through the heather moorland. As you reach the top of the slope the ground can be wet, but very soon you join the road.

Heath Spotted Orchid

5 Turn left and follow it to the end. Pass through a gate and drop down the slope to cross another wet area, then walk on to join the access track to Ward Hill (742ft/258m). It supports a television and radio station but you might be tempted to climb to the top from where, on a good day, you can see all of Shetland. Return to the first cross of tracks and turn left to walk downhill to a wall. Bear left to South Ham and then right to join the road. Stroll left the quiet mile and half to the lighthouse, enjoying the colourful array of wild flowers that fill the verges and ditches.

Practicals

Type of walk: *An excellent trek with some road walking – never unpleasant in Shetland.*

Distance:	9 miles/15km
Time:	5 hours
Maps:	OS Explorer 466/Landranger 4

37

Noss

Park your car at the top of the last hill overlooking the lovely island of Noss, grid ref 528411. Access this by the ro-ro ferry from Lerwick to Bressay then follow the signpost directions for Noss. Walk down the steepish track to climb down steps onto a small jetty. Wait here for an inflatable dinghy (small fee) to come across the narrow Noss Sound. No dogs are allowed on the inflatable. The warden is most vigilant and your waiting time is short. If the Sound is too rough for a crossing a red flag is flown. Check by free phone 0800 107 7818 about operation dates and times. (In 2012 the island closed on August 31st). For mobile phones omit the first 0. Make sure you have suitable clothing and wear strong shoes or boots – the rocks and steps can be slippery when clambering into and out of the boat.

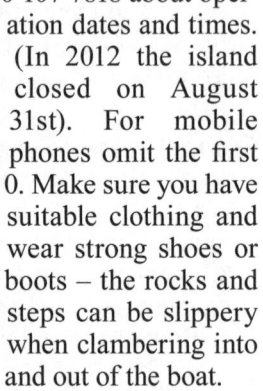

The island is owned by the Garth Estate, and jointly managed by **Scottish Natural Heritage**. The rocks of the island are Old Red Sandstone and this lies horizontally on the cliffs. As these

Cradle Holm, Noss

rocks weather, innumerable ledges are created, just right for the birds to nest and close to their feeding grounds. Here thrive innumerable gannets, fulmars, kittiwakes and guillemots. You will also see many puffins, shags, black guillemots, golden plover, ringed plover and ravens. On the heather moorland great skuas rule, often in conflict with their smaller cousins the arctic skuas.

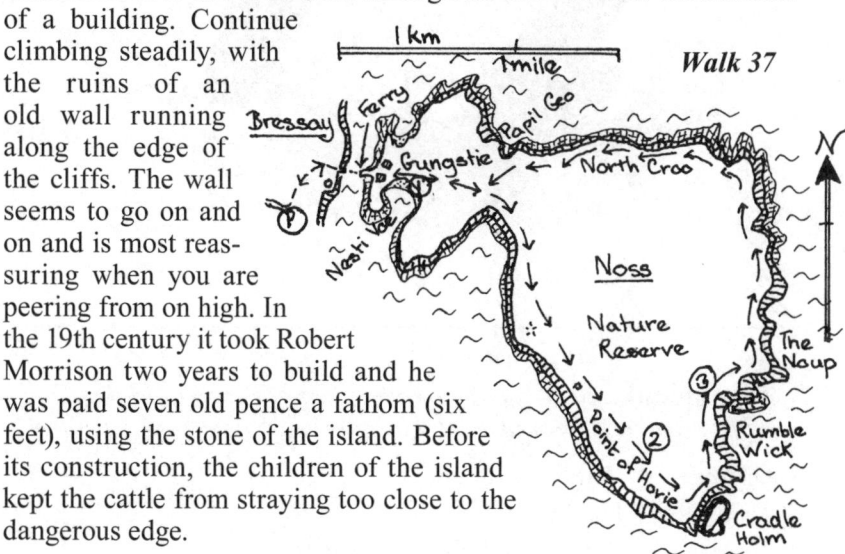

Raven

The house used by the warden and his staff is called **Gungstie** and dates from the 17th century. The buildings were leased by the Marquis of Londonderry to breed Shetland pony stallions used in his coal mines after the 1842 Act of Parliament banned children and women from working there. The island has been inhabited for 4,000 years. The Vikings arrived in the ninth century and the name Noss comes from the Norse for 'a point of rock'. The Jamieson family lived on the island from 1904 to 1939, Noss's last permanent residents.

1 Leave the visitor centre and walk round the lovely sandy bay of Nesti Voe. Strike diagonally right towards the turf dyke and continue to the ladderstile over the wall. Pass through an old wall and the remains of a building. Continue climbing steadily, with the ruins of an old wall running along the edge of the cliffs. The wall seems to go on and on and is most reassuring when you are peering from on high. In the 19th century it took Robert Morrison two years to build and he was paid seven old pence a fathom (six feet), using the stone of the island. Before its construction, the children of the island kept the cattle from straying too close to the dangerous edge.

Walk 37

2 Continue round the Point of Hovie to start climbing to Cradle Holm, a huge grassy-topped stack where a 'cradle' on two cables was used to carry men and sheep across. Others used the cradle to collect eggs and feathers. The contraption was removed in 1864. As you walk on along the cliffs look for the Shetland wren nesting in the wall. Walk on round Charlie's Holm, the top of the stack pitted with puffin burrows. Then as you move on the great gannetry on Rumble Wick and The Noup comes into view. Stay and watch for as long as you can stand the smell.

3 Keep beside the wall to reach the trig point on the Noup (592 ft/181m). From here you can see Unst, Fetlar, Yell, Whalsay, Bressay and Mainland. Then begin the gradual but unrelenting descent to pass several dramatic geos, all packed with guillemots and fulmars. Look for the lovely roseroot colouring the cliff face. Follow the footpath sign, which directs you away from a very contorted red sandstone geo and carry on along North Croo. Climb the ladderstile and follow the wall, keeping north of the Hill of Papilgeo. Cross Hill Dyke to pick up your outward path to the visitor centre.

Razorbills

Practicals

Type of walk: *Easy walking but immense care is required on the cliffs. A magnificent walk with glorious views and much birdlife.*

Distance: 4–5 miles/7–8km
Time: 3 hours
Maps: OS Explorer 466/Landranger 4

38

Mousa Broch

Park at the cobbled pier at Leebitten, grid ref 437249. To access this leave Lerwick by the A970, southbound. After 15 miles, turn left at the sign for Sandwick, Hoswick and the Mousa ferry. Continue down the narrow road for half a mile to the pier. On the short boat journey look out for porpoises and the occasional otter, minke and killer whale. Groups of seabirds seen include guillemots, shags, black guillemots, razorbills, puffins and many gannets fishing.

A regular summer boat service is operated, weather permitting. Telephone 01595 859 674 (to book, the evening before, and to confirm that the trip is possible on the day). The trip on the M/B Solan IV, takes 15 minutes.

Mousa Broch

The broch is one of the **tall drystone hollow-wall towers** unique to Scotland, built by Iron-age farmers about 2,000 years ago, It is extremely well preserved and stands near to its original height of 43 ft, startlingly high when you stand inside and look up. It may have been built as an occasional strong point for the local community, but the small chambers inside suggest that it was later made into a dwelling. The chambers are arranged around a pool of water. There are galleries, an internal staircase, which you can climb, and a parapet. Torches are provided in a cupboard inside the entrance.

In the 18th century, **11 families** lived on the isle, but the last residents left in 1860s. The broch has had two famous couples as tenants. In AD 900 a couple eloping from Norway to Iceland were shipwrecked on the island. They married and spent the winter in the broch. The other couple, the mother of Harald, Earl of Orkney, and her lover, took refuge in the broch and the furious earl laid siege to it, unsuccessfully. He eventually gave up and went away.

In mid summer the broch is wonderfully peaceful and the only tenants are the **storm petrels.** The strange churring noise you may hear, at the right time of the year, is the song of the nestlings. These tiny swallow-like birds, which are well adapted to life at sea, are not agile on land. They can come ashore only after sunset, to brood their young, safe from predation by gulls and skuas.

Storm Petrels

1 Leave the boat and head south (right) over blue squill and tormentil. As you pass a huge boulder beach you are asked to use the board walk behind the beach because the petrels nest between the boulders and are

Walk 38

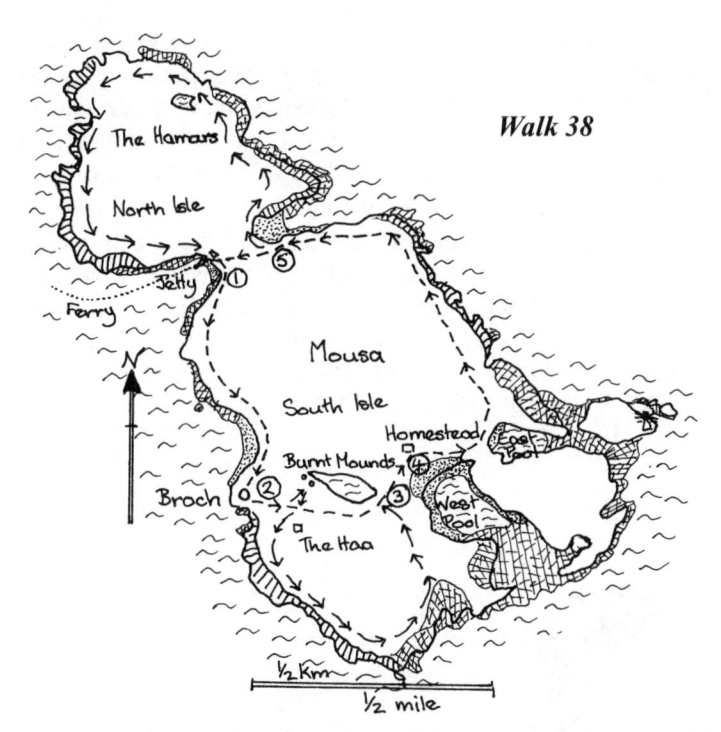

very sensitive to interference. They will desert their eggs or chicks if disturbed. Then visit the broch and wander at will and be amazed.

2 From the broch walk inland to the nearest point of a small loch to see a burnt mound. Return to the coast to walk the magnificent coastline, where red sandstone tilts towards the sea. Continue over a small hill. Further on you come to an area where much sandstone has been removed for paving stones in Lerwick. The builders of the broch used sandstone from the same site.

3 In the breeding season at the tidal West Pool, with a beach of shell-sand, keep inland to avoid disturbing the seals. In the damp hinterland of the pool grow heath spotted orchids and masses of primroses and among these a colony of arctic terns nest. Tread warily because egg and chicks are difficult to spot. Walk with your map on your head to protect yourself from the aerial attacks of these ferocious protectors of their young.

4 When you reach a wall follow it inland to visit the site of an old settlement. You can just see the stones that delineated a passage between two dwellings. Return to West Pool and then continue on to East Pool, keeping behind the wall following waymarked posts, from where you

can watch the seals without disturbing them. Beyond the lovely bay, walk out to look over Bard Sound and glimpse Mousa lighthouse with its jetty. Dawdle on along the cliffs where you might see a huge raft of male eiders. Take care as you round a natural arch-cum-blowhole on the landward side of a deep geo – the waymarked path goes well above it and then through a gap in the wall.

5. Just before you stroll around East Ham onto the North Isle, look for black guillemots on the boulders, close to the water. Here, too, shags dry their wings. Walk along the stone causeway at the edge of the boulder beach. If you are running short of time, follow the path that cuts across the island to the jetty. Otherwise carry on around the cliffs of North Isle, taking care as you pass the tern colonies, to reach the jetty from the north.

Shag

Practicals

Type of walk: *A must for every visitor to Shetland but don't miss the return boat as there is no shelter on the island.*

Distance:	4 miles/6.5km
Time:	All the time between boats
Maps:	OS Explorer 466/Landranger 4

39

Six brochs

This unusual walk takes you along the south-east coast of Mainland, from where you can see or visit six brochs. If you make use of the excellent bus service you can add two more. If you use two cars there is parking at the Crofthouse Museum, grid ref 398147 and at Jarlshof or Scatness at grid ref 389107.

Brochs are believed to have been constructed during the last two centuries BC and the first century AD. It is thought they were built for living in and not as a refuge in times of attack. There is also a theory that they may have been watchtowers as each is in view of the next one. Most had two or more storeys built of wood inside the double stone outer wall, with a single low entrance. The roofs were probably conical in shape and thatched with straw, heather or perhaps even turf.

Clickimin Broch, Lerwick

1. Alight from the bus at the road leading to the Crofthouse Museum, South Voe, Dunrossness. Walk down the lane until you reach the stone-walled thatched crofthouse, a delight to visit, with many original furnishings. Then set out along the cobbled track to the well-preserved little mill built over a small burn. Return across the stream and strike towards the shore, crossing a ladderstile over a wall. Pause as you go to look north, across the Voe towards Outvoe, to a knoll quite close to the sea. Here stand the remnants of the first of the brochs seen on this walk. Closer at hand, just north of the museum, is another hillock, the site of the second broch.

2. Continue south, crossing walls by stiles and then climbing steadily along the sea side of a fence, passing Scarfi Taing and Lambhoga Head. As you near the Point of Blo-geo and Swart Skerry you reach the third broch, with small walled chambers intact. Carry on to pass the enormously long tilting Devonian sandstone that 'walls' a geo. Then cross a small stream and look right to a see a ruined watermill and listen for wrens singing from the undergrowth. Climb a little to where you can spot Sumburgh airport. The pathless way continues right of a wall, with two more fences to cross. Carry on to a gate that gives access to a narrow road. From here Sumburgh Head looms upwards across the Pool of Virkie. Turn right to walk beside the large sea water pool, and look across to a ruined house on a hill. The old dwelling is sited on the fourth broch of the walk.

Walk 39

3   Press on to join the A970. Turn left and walk for 2.5km. Just after the airport runway, which you should cross with care, look left for the excavations at Scatness. The ruins, part of which date from the Bronze Age, were revealed when the new road was cut. They are being slowly and carefully excavated. In the centre of the site stands the fifth broch of the walk, standing 5 ft high. There are viewing platforms and visitor facilities. Carry on along the A-road to take the right turn to Sumburgh Hotel and the entrance to Jarlshof. Stroll through the magnificent site (see walk 2) to see the thick walls of the sixth broch. Climb the viewing platform for a marvellous view of the site.

4   To return to Lerwick, pick up the bus from the road end. As the bus turns off the A-road towards Sandwick, look across Mousa Sound to see the island of Mousa and your seventh superb broch (walk 38). On nearing Lerwick, it's worth alighting from the bus at the Clickimin Broch and wandering round this stunning site – your eighth broch.

Skylark

Practicals

Type of walk: *This pathless walk along the dramatic cliffs is full of interest. It lends itself to using public transport. Take Leasks bus from Lerwick, perhaps the 9.30 from the bus station in Commercial Street.*

Distance:	6¼ miles/10km
Time:	3–4 hours
Maps:	OS Explorer 466/ Landranger 4

40

Fair Isle

There are two ways of reaching this beautiful island, either by boat or plane. For details of the boat crossings contact 01595 760363. There is only one sailing, so be prepared to stay on the island for a couple of nights. Alternatively take the inter-island flight from Tingwall Airport for a return trip. Contact for times 01595 840246. There is hostel accommodation at the Bird Observatory.

Fair Isle, three miles long and a mile wide, lies 23 miles from Sumburgh Head. In 1948 the island was bought by the ornithologist George Waterston. He thus achieved a dream that had helped him survive the rigours of being a prisoner of war. In 1954 he handed over the island to the National Trust for Scotland, who still own it.

On the **cliff edge below the lighthouse** sit, with care, and watch the many birds. Puffins will sit close to your feet. Fulmars fill almost every ledge on the sandstone cliff face. Guillemots, by the hundreds, stand in line with faces to the wall on the ledges far down. Razorbills find gaps between the latter. Shags fly to the lower darker part of the great cliffs. Out on a great white stack and just off the cliffs there is a

Sheep Craig, Fair Isle

large gannetry, which began to form in 1975. There is constant movement as an enormous number of birds fly to and from their nest sites and their rich feeding grounds out at sea. Fair Isle is also noted for the large variety of unusual migrant birds that make landfall there in spring and autumn.

1 The plane lands on an airstrip used during the Second World War. There is a waiting room and toilet. Walk round the perimeter until opposite the facilities and begin the long climb up a reinforced track. This comes to a very obvious British Telecom mast, built on the site of an old crofthouse. From here follow a grassy groove straight to the top of Ward hill (712ft/217m), where stands a walled trig point. Enjoy the wonderful view of the whole island and of Sumburgh Head, Fitful Head, Bressay and Noss. Here men watched for the dreaded press gang, racing off to hide in caves on Malcolm's Head, facing Fogli Stack. Later men watched for U-boats in the First World War.

2 Walk north, right, with care along the cliffs, then drop down the slope, east, in the direction of the north lighthouse across the mossy turf. Cross the Burn of Wirrve on concrete blocks and climb up between two small hills. Continue to a tiny lochan and walk right beside the pool and the remains of the old north-south dyke, an ancient wall. Continue on to a narrow road, turn left and dawdle past the black Golden Water, where tufted ducks idle. Carry on along the road to pass a great blowhole, linked to the sea by a long subterranean passage.

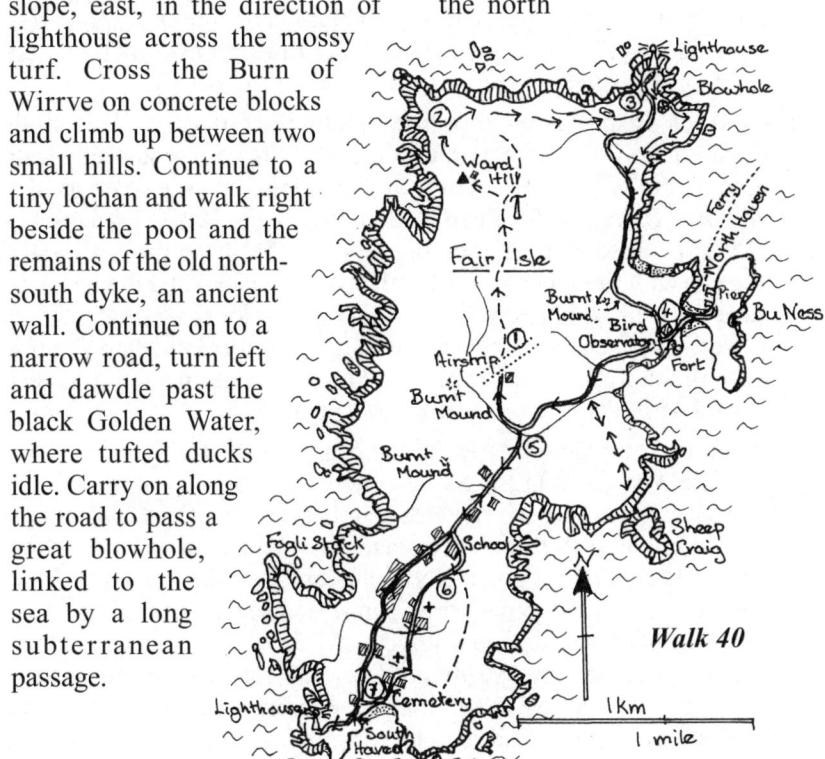

Walk 40

3 Before the lighthouse, stride over, warily, to the edge of the cliffs to see many of Fair Isle's sea birds. Return to the road and continue, right, up to the lighthouse, built in 1891; now fully automated, the houses empty. Then begin to walk south, along the lovely cliffs or down the road. As the road winds round left, walk inland to Ferni-cup to see two burnt mounds, part of what is believed to be a Bronze Age settlement. Return to the road and stride on. Round the next corner you reach the bird observatory. Continue behind it to visit a glorious stretch of sand at North Haven. Here you might see the Good Shepherd IV in her giant noust blasted out of the side of Bu Ness, and the breakwater protecting the small harbour, where you might have landed if you reached the island by boat.

4 Return past the observatory and make a detour to see, on a promontory, an early Iron-Age fort with ramparts guarding its entrance. Go on to pass many of the nets used by the observatory for ringing and data collection. Look left, cross the stile and walk over to see Sheep Craig (444ft/132m); the huge grass-topped stack is linked to the island by an isthmus. Sheep and men were once winched by chains to its smooth turf. Head on along the road and then on your right is a quick return to the airstrip. Hopefully you have more time left to stroll towards the south of the island where the Fair Islanders live.

5 Go on along the narrow road and look for the hill dyke, a long straight drystone wall that almost divides the island in two, separating heather moor to the north and the crofts and green fields to the south. Beside it you can see traces of a much older dyke, 'Feelie Dyke', with remnants of turf-covered stone. Stride on between the sheep pastures and the occasional tethered cow. Where the road divides, take the left fork to pass the well-equipped school, which caters for pupils until they are 11 year old. Beside the school is the Community Hall. Here you might have time to join in with their various activities including a weekly workshop of the Fair Isle Crafts Co-operative.

6 Head on along the road to visit the beautifully refurbished Church of Scotland kirk, built in 1892. Close by, on its hill, and installed in 1982, is an aero-generator, which helps supply electricity for the isle. Further on you might wish to visit the Methodist chapel, another lovely quiet haven. Behind the chapel is the old school building, which houses the George Waterston memorial centre and the museum. Here are the archives, photographs and artefacts of Fair Isle's past, some inspiring and some depressing. Stride on down the road to the immaculately kept walled graveyard where there is a sunny bench seat. Some of the headstones make for sad reading. Look for the iron cross to the right

of the gate, which commemorates the wreck, in 1588, of the El Gran Grifon, the flagship of the defeated Armada. More than 300 survivors were landed on the isle to be supported by 17 households living at subsistence level. Over 50 Spaniards died of starvation. In 1984 the Spanish came again to dedicate the cross in the kirkyard.

7 Continue along the road, through a gate, to pass the Puffin, an old fish store, since 1976 a hostel used by school children and people from the observatory. Here sheep on the shore feed on seaweed. Nearby are old boat nousts and flat stones for drying fish. Here too, is South Haven pier, which has to be approached past skerries and small stacks – rather more perilous than the North Haven harbour. Return past the Puffin to visit the taller South Light, which has a brilliant white and yellow accommodation block . Return along the road and where it divides, keep to the left branch. Climb the hill to pass a crofthouse with an old kiln used for drying corn and oats. Keep climbing to pass the well-stocked shop, where you can buy postcards and there is a toilet. Stride along the road, remembering to take the left turn to the airstrip.

Arctic Skua

Practicals

Type of walk: *A magical day's walking. A steep climb to the top of Ward Hill.*

Distance: 8 miles/13km
Time: The time between flights or boats
Maps: OS Explorer 466/Landranger 4

Walking Scotland Series
from Clan Books

MARY WELSH AND CHRISTINE ISHERWOOD have completed this series of guides covering the whole of Scotland's mainland and principal islands.

Full list of volumes available:
1. WALKING THE ISLE OF ARRAN
2. WALKING THE ISLE OF SKYE
3. WALKING WESTER ROSS
4. WALKING PERTHSHIRE
5. WALKING THE WESTERN ISLES
6. WALKING ORKNEY
7. WALKING SHETLAND
8. WALKING THE ISLES OF ISLAY, JURA AND COLONSAY
9. WALKING GLENFINNAN: THE ROAD TO THE ISLES
10. WALKING THE ISLES OF MULL, IONA, COLL AND TIREE
11. WALKING DUMFRIES AND GALLOWAY
12. WALKING ARGYLL AND BUTE
13. WALKING DEESIDE, DONSIDE AND ANGUS
14. WALKING THE TROSSACHS, LOCH LOMONDSIDE AND THE CAMPSIE FELLS
15. WALKING GLENCOE, LOCHABER AND THE GREAT GLEN
16. WALKING STRATHSPEY, MORAY, BANFF AND BUCHAN
17. WALKING AROUND LOCH NESS, THE BLACK ISLE AND EASTER ROSS
18. WALKING CAITHNESS AND SUTHERLAND
19. WALKING THE SCOTTISH BORDERS AND EAST LOTHIAN
20. WALKING AYRSHIRE, RENFREWSHIRE AND LANARKSHIRE
21. WALKING FIFE, THE OCHILS, TAYSIDE AND THE FORTH VALLEY

Books in this series can be ordered through booksellers anywhere. In the event of difficulty write to
Clan Books, The Cross, DOUNE, FK16 6BE, Scotland.

For more details, visit the Clan Books website at
www.walkingscotlandseries.co.uk